At His Feet

Lessons Learned from the Master

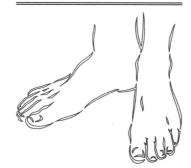

At His Feet

Lessons Learned from the Master

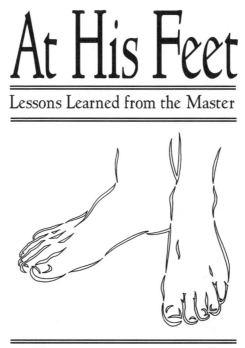

MADGE BECKON

GOSPEL FOLIO PRESS
P. O. Box 2041, Grand Rapids MI 49501-2041

Cover design by J. B. Nicholson, Jr.

Published by Gospel Folio Press
P. O. Box 2041, Grand Rapids, MI 49501-2041

ISBN 1-882701-04-6

Printed in the United States of America

DEDICATION

To my daughters, Ruth, Esther, and Eunice, who have taught me nearly as much as I have taught them. To my two sons-in-law and my granddaughter, Heather, all of whom I love dearly.

To my immediate family and the missionaries with whom I worked who have been there with their support and happy fellowship during the many years.

To the faithful saints whose prayers and support have made the years of service possible. To my equally beloved family of Japanese Christians who may enjoy the English version of *Ashimoto ni Suwatte*.

You are very special people. I thank God for you all.

CONTENTS

ACKNOWLEDGMENTS

I would like to express a large debt of gratitude to Gloria Speechly of the Evangelical Publishing Depot, who first encouraged me to contribute to the *Fujin Memo* (Memos for Housewives). She compiled the articles during eleven years, and in 1986 published them in book form.

Equal thanks goes to my daughter, Esther, who has worked many long hours at the computer in revising the English copies with me. I greatly appreciate her many contributions in the form of ideas and corrections, and it is highly unlikely this book would have been published without her help.

Final thanks goes to Stephen and Amanda Sorenson for their cooperation in the editing of *Missionary Memos*.

It is a joy to have known and enjoyed fellowship with all these dear, devoted saints of the Lord.

PREFACE

At His Feet is the English version of the book, *Ashimoto ni Suwatte*, which was published in Japan in 1986 by Evangelical Publishing Depot of Tokyo. *Ashimoto ni Suwatte* (translated, Sitting at His Feet) is a compilation of short articles I wrote for the women's page of the magazine, *Mikotoba* (God's Word). The first article was written in 1975, shortly after my husband passed away. Many of the articles are rooted in my memories of personal experiences dating back to the time of our leaving the United States for the first time to go to China. A few have been written since my retirement in Denver. Many of them are based on women in the Bible. I wrote them to be a source of strength and a challenge to Japanese Christian women. I pray that they may be as much of an encouragement to you to continue on in the faith and the service of our Lord Jesus Christ as they have been to me in writing them.

Madge Beckon
Englewood, Colorado

1
A HOUSE WITH ALL THE TRIMMINGS

For three consecutive mornings in January, 1986, the Lord impressed on me through three verses from the Book of Genesis that I should return to my family in America. I had a problem believing this could possibly be the will of God because the reasons against returning were numerous. I was enjoying the work the Lord had opened to me in Japan; I owned my own home there; and if I were to return from the mission field, I wouldn't know where to settle in the United States because my family was scattered.

After a week of not being able to shake off the impression that the Lord was leading me to return, I decided to pray about it for a three-month period, not sharing the thought with a single person. I asked God that if the plan could possibly be His, that He would confirm and strengthen the feeling. If it was not His will, I asked Him to decrease my thoughts of going to the United States. By the end of the first three months, Genesis 31:3 was increasingly impressed in my mind: *"Return unto the land of thy fathers, and to thy kindred; and I will be with thee."* I shared my feelings with the elders of the church in Takasaki, Japan, and asked them to pray with me for three more months with the same stipulations. At the end of that three-month period, the assurance I felt had increased to the point that I asked them to share it with the whole church. I, in turn, shared it with my family and friends.

During the summer of that year when I was still undecided, my daughter, Esther, called from Denver to say she had seen a house in Englewood, Colorado. It was not only a "darling house," but was within two blocks of where Eunice, my other daughter, lived. I told her to inquire about the price, but to go no further than that, since I wasn't about to buy a house I had not seen and I wasn't sure I'd leave Japan. However, that problem soon solved itself. The following week, the "for sale" sign was removed from the front yard. The house apparently had been sold.

In September, when the last three-month period ended, I made the decision to return to the United States. The big problem facing me was the sale of my home in Japan. Five years previously, the assembly had purchased a large western-style home for me in exchange for our old family house, which they soon tore down and replaced with a beautiful, new chapel. My new home had been purchased cheaply at a public auction because it had the reputation of being an unlucky house.

I was afraid I had a white elephant on my hands because of its questionable past. I knew the average Japanese would not be interested, so I dreaded even putting it on the market.

As it happened, my worry was in vain. One afternoon, a missionary's daughter stopped in for a cup of tea, a chat, and a time of prayer. As a prayer request, I told her about my concern in selling the house. She promised to pray with me about it. She went home that evening and told her husband about the house. Within three days, they came to see the place. He immediately liked the unusual modern design and decided to buy it for a teacher who was coming from the U.S. to teach English in his school. The Lord spared me the trouble of even having to clean the place for a showing or an open house. I was free to tell my daughters in Denver to line up houses for me to look at when I returned to the States, and I began packing in earnest. I had no problem disposing of my household items. I shipped my personal belongings and left Japan on Thursday, January 16, 1987, arriving in Denver the same day.

On Saturday morning, Eunice received a phone call from a

real estate agent, who asked if we were still interested in the house on Clarkson Street. This was the same house that Esther had liked so much, from the outside, when she walked through the neighborhood months earlier. You can imagine the excitement with which Eunice answered that we certainly were. As a family we went right over immediately and my son-in-law, in the construction business, told me that it was well-built.

Our whole family had the "this is it" feeling about the house. However, I told the owner and the agent that although I was truly interested, I needed the weekend to pray about my decision. This brought about an unexpected response, "I identify with that." We left with the promise to return on Tuesday morning with our answer. After seeing the place one more time, we were more convinced than ever that it was just the house God had prepared for me. It had a large living room for Bible classes and was close enough for Eunice and her family to walk over for a cup of tea anytime.

As I left the house, the agent asked me, "When will your furniture arrive from Japan?" I told her I had nothing coming from Japan, that everything I owned was stacked in boxes in one room in Eunice's basement. This statement caused unexpected excitement from the agent. She invited us to come back into the house, seated us at the dining room table and told us the owners wanted to leave all the furnishings in the house. The owner handed us a list of all the furnishings, including washer, dryer, microwave, stereo, and all garden equipment. Within minutes we came to an agreement that they would leave everything in the house as it was except for their personal things. The owner voluntarily reduced the price of the house, making it possible for me to buy the house and all the furnishings within my budget. Both parties were convinced that the Lord had a strong hand in this transaction.

On the closing date, the previous owner's wife and I sat at the table and our tears flowed unashamedly. She was so glad that someone who would appreciate their beloved home and make good use of it was moving in, and I was glad to be that person. They moved out one day; Esther and I moved in the next. We were surprised and pleased to find that the lady had left three beds completely made up with sheets, pillows, blankets, and bedspreads.

After we had been in the house about a month, a friend asked, "Are you feeling settled yet?" I told her that I had never felt unsettled. Once again the Lord proved His love by providing for our every need. We lacked nothing! I didn't even have to spend hours shopping for used furniture at garage sales as I had imagined I would.

So it was with the ancient people of God in their wilderness journey: *"At the commandment of the Lord they rested in the tents, and at the commandment of the Lord they journeyed"* (Num. 9:23).

2
AND SO ARE THE TURKEYS

I guess one sign of advancing age is the rapidity with which the mind reverts to bygone days. This happened to me recently when I read, *"The cattle upon a thousand hills are mine"* (Ps. 50:9-11). I also read a notation I had written next to the text: "And so are the turkeys."

That seemingly odd comment had its source in our second Christmas in Japan. Gifford's parents and his younger brother, who were in Japan at the time, planned to have Christmas dinner with us. As Christmas drew closer, the larder decreased and no funds came in to replenish it. By Christmas Eve, I still didn't have one yen with which to purchase a single food item, and I was expected to prepare Christmas dinner for seven!

As the sky darkened at the end of the day, so did my spirits. I became more anxious because I didn't want to disappoint my guests and it looked as if the Lord was going to let us down. Yet Gifford went on with his duties in a perfectly normal way, fully expecting the Lord to supply our needs in time. I wasn't quite so sure the Lord would provide and the calmness with which Gifford accepted the situation made it even more aggravating to me. After all, I was the one who had to put the food on the table.

At six in the evening, I heard a tap on the kitchen door and opened it. With an embarrassed look, a fellow missionary handed me an envelope, wished me a "Merry Christmas," and was gone. Opening it, I found a one-thousand yen bill enclosed. Overwhelmed with emotion, I could only stand in my doorway, watching him disappear. I felt thankfulness, shame, and rebuke all at the same moment.

Leaving the children with Gifford, I went into town. On the way, I made a mental list of what I could buy with the thousand yen. To this day, I don't know how I concluded that all the trimmings for a Christmas dinner were the best buy, but I did. I bought everything except meat. (A thousand yen just wasn't enough to buy meat for seven people).

The return bicycle trip was invigorating, to say nothing of the joy of having a full basket of food. I had only been home a few minutes when I heard a "Gomen kudasai" ("Excuse me"), this time at the front door. I glanced at the clock and wondered who would be there at 8:30 on Christmas Eve. Can you imagine the look on my face when I opened the door to see one of our English Bible class students standing there with a live turkey? He was grinning from ear to ear.

I was almost too speechless to invite him in. I didn't even know they raised turkeys in Japan, but he soon explained that he had read a book that said Americans usually ate turkey at Christmas. Inquiring around, he found a poult, which he bought and raised with us in mind. We were deeply touched by his thoughtfulness and love.

God would have been supplying our needs if He'd sent hot dogs, but in His great love for us He sent one of His choicest turkeys. With indescribable joy, we heated water and plucked and stuffed our special gift. The following day, our American guests enjoyed a traditional Christmas dinner—turkey with all the trimmings. Our little girls could hardly believe their eyes. God had provided more than our needs—and He did it through a schoolboy.

3
AN ISRAELITE MOTHER

"And the Lord spake unto Moses, saying, Speak unto the children of Israel, and bid them that they make fringes in the borders of their garments throughout their generations, and that they put ... a ribband of blue..." (Num. 15:37-38). As I read this, I realized how much work was entailed in handsewing ribbons and fringes on every garment for every family member.

This set my imagination to work. I imagined that a mother had just heard Moses' order. Wanting to immediately obey, she positioned a whole stack of clothes in front of her. As she sewed, with her young daughter at her elbow, in my mind I heard the following conversation between them:

"Why blue, Mommy? I like red better. Can God see a little ribbon from heaven? Why does Moses always tell us what to do?"

As the mother answered one question, new ones came. The little girl tried to understand the reasons for all the fuss and extra work, and her mother explained as best she could why God had asked them to do this, being well aware that all her children would be influenced by her reaction and attitude toward God's command. I pictured her trying to help the child work through as many questions as possible.

I then thought about how I would answer if my child asked me why God chose the color blue. Blue, a heavenly color, was to remind the Israelites that they were to be holy, just as God is holy, and that they were God's special people. Whether standing, sitting, or kneeling, they were always able to see the ribbons and the fringes on the hems of their garments. The ribbons reminded them that they were heavenly people, people not of this world. It isn't just that God wanted the Israelites to dress differently. He wanted to remind them that they belonged to Him. We would do well to impress this truth on our children. The God of the heavens is our God, too. We don't necessarily have to dress differently, but we are to keep the fact that we are a holy people on our minds constantly. God is as aware today of the little things as He was then of ribbons and fringes.

Moses was only a mouthpiece; it was really God who gave the commandment. He loved His people just as He loves His children today. He wanted them to wear the ribbons so they would remember that He was responsible for them, just as He wants us to remember that He cares for us today.

Going back to the fanciful story, I imagined the mother also telling her daughter that if God had not used Moses to bring them out of Egypt, she would have been a little slave girl at that very moment. The mother no doubt would shudder, knowing all too well what that implied. The very thought of what she and her family had been delivered from would give her fingers fresh energy and she would gladly continue with appreciation to sew the blue ribbon and fringe on each garment in the pile.

Knowing that our children pick up our attitudes, we need to constantly have fresh thoughts about God and, as Paul encouraged the Corinthian believers to bring their thought-life into captivity to Christ (2 Cor. 10:5), we should remind our children to do likewise. There are many influences in the world about us today that will quickly corrupt their minds and draw them away from the simplicity which is found in Christ Jesus if they are not taught to be on guard against them (see 2 Cor. 11:3). Therefore, we should be careful to teach our children to unashamedly and willingly wear thoughts from God's Word as they would blue ribbons on their spiritual garments.

4
A STORY OF TWO PAUPERS

I have many favorite Bible stories, but the story of the widow in 2 Kings 4:1-7 has been a favorite of favorites for years, especially now that I am a widow. The dear widow in this story was poor. When her husband died, she was left with a large debt. The creditor came to take her two sons away from her and turn them into his slaves. She had lost her primary means of support when her husband died, and if her boys were taken away, her future security would go as well. Understandably she was desperate. She didn't have adequate food in the house, not even enough for a few days. She was down to just one little pot of oil. In every sense of the word, she was a pauper.

I had an aunt who lived and died as a pauper. I have fond memories of her. When I was a child, I loved her dearly. She was the youngest member of the family and single, so when my grandparents became ill, her brothers and sisters decided that she would assume responsibility for their parents' care, and that she should inherit their eighty-acre homestead on the outskirts of a major city.

During the depression, times were difficult for my aunt and my grandparents. By the time the depression ended, she had formed such a habit of poverty that she never was able to free herself from her "poor" complex. Because of the required time and cost of caring for her parents, she had no income and lost her savings in the depression. In time, my grandparents passed away, the city surrounded the farm on all sides and the property value went up greatly. Real estate agents came to buy parts of her land, but she couldn't bring herself to sell any of the family property. So she continued to live in poverty. She never availed herself of modern conveniences, thinking they were too extravagant. She didn't even eat properly because she didn't have cash on hand for nourishing food. No matter how many members of the family tried to persuade her, she would not sell even one small lot, the price of which would have provided a stable income. She lived and died as a pauper because she did not use the source of income at her disposal. Foolishly she never enjoyed what was hers. What a pity!

In contrast, the widow of 2 Kings 4 was also a poor woman, but there wasn't anything she could do to help herself. She was a pauper in reality, while my aunt was a pauper only in her imagination. But the results of their poverty were the same: need, inadequacy, and inferiority. However, there was a crucial difference between these women. One chose to stay in poverty while the other sought help from God. One refused advice while the other acted in obedience to a directive from a man of God.

My aunt reminds me of many who continue to live in spiritual poverty just because they are afraid to step out in faith. They live and die in spiritual defeat, filled with feelings of inadequacy and inferiority, even though all the resources of Almighty God are theirs in Christ Jesus. In contrast, the widow, in complete obedience to Elisha, picked up the pot of oil and began pouring its oil into other empty vessels. But the real test of her faith was proven earlier, when she began to gather the pots from the whole neighborhood.

We already have the Holy Spirit, (typified by the oil) living within us and have the possibility of using all the treasures hidden in Christ Jesus to enjoy blessed and meaningful lives. All we need to do is share these treasures with others. Let's begin to pour out what we have, drawing from His endless supply. Let us enjoy rich, full, and happy Christian lives!

5
A Widow Makes a Hard Choice

In reading the wonderful stories in Scripture, I find it easy to take situations like the one in 1 Kings 17:8-16 for granted. It seems natural for Bible characters to do self-sacrificing things, but when I try to imagine myself in their shoes, I realize what great people they really were. One such person was the widow of Zarephath.

God put this dear woman in a tough place. She had to decide whether to take the food out of the mouth of her own flesh and blood to give it to another or to feed her hungry son. When Elijah suddenly appeared out of nowhere, he told her, *"Bring me, I pray thee, a morsel of bread."* When she explained her dire circumstances and told him that they were literally starving, he didn't change his request. In fact, he made things even more difficult by telling her to bake the bread and to give it to him "first." He didn't ask her to divide it between him and the boy; he asked for all of it.

The amazing thing is that she actually baked the bread and gave it to Elijah first, just as he asked her to do. I don't think this came naturally for her, any more than it would have been for me. I would have struggled hard and long before being willing to use my last bit of oil and flour to bake a pancake for a complete stranger—and then feed him first!

It's one thing for a person who has been walking in total dependence on God to go one step further in faith, but we have no reason to believe that she—just an ordinary, poor housewife—had any previous experiences along this line. Verse 9 indicates that God had told her that He would send someone for her to care for, but He evidently hadn't given her the details as to how she would do it. When Elijah actually arrived, it seemed impossible that she could serve him because she had nothing with which to make a meal. Surely disappointed and most likely puzzled, she used her last bit of flour and oil to make a pancake and gave it to Elijah "first" in total obedience.

In trying to find the lesson in this story, I have come to the conclusion that the emphasis is on the word "first." At issue is the chronological timing rather than what or who is more important. In discerning the Lord's will, we must take His timing into consideration as well as His instructions.

It would have been just as easy for God to have filled the widow's barrel with flour and her pot with oil before Elijah arrived as it was to do it the slow way. But God used His own methods, wanting to prove to her that He was alive and vitally interested in her plight. Elijah's main message was that God lives, and through her own experience she had the opportunity to learn this great truth. Think of her delight as, three times a day, she saw the miracle of the flour and the oil being replenished.

In our day, too, the more difficult the demand that God makes, the greater is the assurance that He is still alive when we see Him provide. It seems that the tougher the test, the greater the joy when we obey. Perhaps this is the reason that the older we get in the faith, the more challenging our tests become. Sometimes we have to follow in faith and fit in with God's timing even when nothing makes sense to us.

One Sunday afternoon, three other women and I had an unusual burden to visit a dear sister who was suffering from terminal cancer. I wanted to go, but I had a problem. Knowing I had only five dollars in my purse and that I had planned to stop on the way home to shop for something for our breakfast, I didn't see how I could bring my friend the usual gift that Japanese culture required.

Reluctantly, I decided to go and called first to see if there was anything in particular that our friend would like. Her husband quickly responded that she had mentioned that honeydew melon was the only food she had been able to retain. So we decided to buy a honeydew melon and share the cost even though they were out of season and cost between twenty and twenty-five dollars each, making my share at least five dollars. I wouldn't dare admit to you what went through my mind as I gave my friends the precious five dollars. In my mind this meant that my family would not have breakfast.

We had a lovely visit. Our sister in Christ and her whole family (they were all unsaved) were grateful for the fruit. She enjoyed what little she ate. As I dropped one of the ladies off at her house on my way home, she asked me to wait a minute. When she reappeared, she handed me a carton of eggs. I had to blink to keep back the tears as I thanked her and drove off. Why eggs? Yes, breakfast, remember?

Imagine the sensation that went through me the following evening when the news came that our sister had gone to be with the Lord. I was left with the supreme memory of having a share in giving her one last taste of honeydew melon. It was a decision I have not regretted. If my own joy was that great when God provided eggs for our breakfast, I can imagine the thrill the widow in 1 Kings experienced day after day when she saw God replenish flour and oil to meet her needs. I know she doesn't have any regrets, either.

6

A Wife's Influence in the Church

Few women fully realize how much their influence is felt in the Church of God. I'm sure Job's wife didn't when she cried out in the desperation of her frustration, *"Curse God, and die"*! (Job 2:9). How was she to know that what she said in the privacy of her home would be read and repeated in gatherings of believers through the ages and in nearly every country of the world?

Fortunately, Job was strong enough spiritually to withstand this fiery dart, but not all men are. Even though he resisted her words at the time, I wonder if perhaps his slip into despair afterward and his longing for death were not the result of her evil suggestion to end it all. We have to admit that a spirit such as hers is catching. It only takes a seed of thought to reap an action.

The Lord has used an experience that happened to me one Sunday morning years ago. Many times it has helped me to check what I say. That morning, for some reason, I woke up on the wrong side of the bed. I was at odds with the world. I expressed my bad mood at the breakfast table by saying some very unkind words to Gifford. In this unpleasant atmosphere, we left the house for the Lord's Supper. On the way, Gifford was preoccupied by the previous conversation and unwittingly ran a red light. Fortunately the streets were nearly clear at that hour—except for a traffic policeman who soon waved us over. He scolded Gifford in a tone no kinder than mine had been. The rest of our journey was made in dead silence. Even the three little girls in the back seat were quiet!

My husband was a guest speaker that morning, but everything he said and did lacked power, for it came from a heavy, grieved heart. The lips that were always ready to thank and praise the Lord gave the morning message as if only out of duty. The man who usually had trouble closing a message on time finished early. I blamed him in my heart for a lack of preparation, while all the time his failure was the result of a poor spirit I had created.

We were invited out for dinner, but Gifford was unusually quiet. His silence only agitated me, so I talked more to cover up for him. Needless to say, neither of us really enjoyed our dinner, nor were we a spiritual blessing to our hosts.

Later, in the quietness of our home when we could talk things over and pray quietly together, God showed me how greatly I had influenced our day because I had permitted a bad mood to generate a family spat. My influence on Gifford that morning had robbed God of His due praise and also robbed the saints of being fed properly. It was really my fault that the time of fellowship with the Christian family we visited that day was of no spiritual profit. I had affected our whole day and, worse, had influenced Gifford's testimony.

Since that experience, I can understand why Paul included instructions to wives when he admonished Timothy in how to establish a church. God knows how greatly we wives can encourage or discourage our husbands. Gifford often confided to me that he could take opposition from outside sources, but found it next to impossible to fight against a disapproving and critical spirit within the home. As a result, I prayed hundreds of times, "Lord, if I can't be a positive influence, at least keep me from hindering my husband in his work for Thee" (especially on Sunday morning).

May we wives, being aware of our influence, consider our husbands and thus: *"Provoke unto love and to good works"* (Heb. 10:24) and function *"...as being heirs together of the grace of life; that [our] prayers be not hindered"* (1 Peter 3:7).

7
BACA, VALLEY OF TEARS

I'm happy to be a woman when I realize that the Lord of heaven and earth revealed some of His most profound truths to women. By doing so, He expressed His faith and trust in womanhood. Let me name four women whose experiences in faith have challenged me at various times: Anna, Mary and, Martha, and the Samaritan woman. These women, despite their varied backgrounds and social standing, had one common denominator: sorrow. They all had known the bitter disappointment of cherished dreams as they passed through the Valley of Tears.

Anna's husband died while she was very young. However, she did not stay in that Valley. Although continuing to experience loneliness and the reproach of widowhood, she completed a long, full life of service while waiting for the Messiah. This may be the secret of her discernment. Many hours in fellowship with God through prayer, without doubt, had prepared her heart for the special revelation concerning Christ.

The Lord revealed to Anna that God's Messiah had actually come into the world as a tiny baby. She was one of the first people to recognize that the wonderful truth of the Old Testament prophecies concerning a promised Saviour had finally been fulfilled. The Holy Spirit gave her the assurance that this was He! She immediately went out to tell others with whom she had been sharing her hope (see Luke 2:36-38). I covet her recognition and assurance of who He is.

Mary's devotion to Christ evidences that she realized the life from which she had been saved. Only those who are aware of the misery of a sinful life can appreciate, as Mary did, the greatness of the Saviour. Those who are forgiven much love much, and Mary loved much. She came out victoriously (John 12:3-8).

Mary was apparently the only person who grasped the fact of Christ's substitutionary death on the cross, even though Christ had spoken repeatedly and clearly of His crucifixion. She risked being criticized and, at great personal sacrifice, went into action by preparing Him for His burial while He was still alive. The Lord praised her for her devotion; how much it meant to Him in the shadow of the cross (see John 12:3-8). I covet her comprehension and ability to glorify Christ.

Martha knew the bitterness of tears when Lazarus, her brother and her security, died, but she also turned her valley of bewilderment and confusion into a well of resurrected life in Christ. Through her encounter with Christ, backed up by obedience to His command, she had the joy of seeing the Lord raise her brother from the dead.

To Martha was given the truth of the Resurrection and the promise that, if she would believe, she would see the glory of God (see John 11:40). Christ caused her to look beyond death into life eternal by assuring her that He Himself was Life, thus teaching her that as the source of life itself, He had the power to rescue humanity from the grave (John 11:25). I long for such faith, which looks beyond the crushing need to the triumph available in the Saviour.

The woman at Jacob's well had lived through the tears of five broken marriages. She must have been deeply disappointed with life. But at Christ's invitation she drank from the well of cleansing water that flowed out into the healing joy of forgiveness. She also turned her valley of shame into a wellspring of blessing for others. She forgot herself. Her newfound joy and adoration of Christ soon invigorated her to become an effective witness to the whole city.

Christ taught this unnamed Samaritan woman at Jacob's well the importance of true worship (John 4:23-26). It is amazing that the Lord explained to a woman (and a Samaritan woman at that) the secret that God actually longs for love and worship. While she was still unsaved, Christ gave her a tiny glimpse of the desire God has to be remembered and appreciated. The perception of this teaching gave wings to her feet as she set out to bring others to Him. I covet her spirit of adoration, which produced eagerness and energy for witnessing.

The psalmist expressed the same sentiment all these women had when he wrote, *"Blessed is the man whose strength is in thee; in whose heart are the ways of them. Who passing through the valley of Baca [tears] make it a well; the rain also filleth the pools. They go from strength to strength"* (Psalm 84:5-7). As these women met Christ in a very personal way, they discovered a well in the valley. By drinking constantly of the water that He gave them, they, too, were able to go from one experience to another in His strength.

At one time, the Assyrians said that the God of the Israelites was a God of the hills only, not of the valleys. However, these women proved for themselves that God was the God of the valleys, too, especially the Valley of Tears. In other words, by coming to Christ and drinking the water that He provided, they discovered the secret of a truly fulfilled life. By seeing Christ in a new perspective and permitting God's sunshine to shine through the teardrops, they witnessed a rainbow of His manifold graces. Each victory they had gave joy, and joy in turn gave strength. Thus they, like the psalmist, were enabled to meet each new situation by going from strength to strength, from oasis to oasis through this desert-world.

31

8
BIG DECISIONS, BIG RESULTS

Because of the large part Bible camps had played in his life, Gifford was eager to start one in Japan. For several years, he prayed and planned to build the camp. When we returned to Japan after our first furlough, we felt that we were ready to start and began looking for property. After searching for three years, all the pieces began to fall into place within a four-day period. Plans began to take shape. We found the "perfect" location in the foothills with the right price tag, and we sold two empty lots on either side of our house in the city to finance it.

On the fourth day, we had the money for the youth camp in our possession, but it was too late in the day to deposit it into the bank. So we put it into an unassuming envelope and tucked it under some clothing on a shelf in our clothes closet, thrilled that the camp was at long last going to be a reality.

It turned out that the cash became a great temptation to Gifford. Unknown to me, he had been struggling for a few days with a powerful longing to change cars, since our car was in such poor condition. The door on the passenger side was wired shut because it had flown open twice. This happened once when I was driving an older lady home and could have created a serious accident. He reasoned that this money could be the Lord's provision for a new car instead of the beginning for a youth camp.

A longing to own a new car, a longing that Gifford had had all of his life, was now within reach. The money we had in hand from the sale of our property was legitimately his. He had dreamed about cars ever since he had left Inland China and returned to the United States with his missionary family. As a little boy, he had drawn pictures of cars and imagined himself behind the wheel of every shiny new car he saw.

Our three girls were home from boarding school for a spring break the day we tucked the "camp" money into the closet. I'd been coming down with the flu and had a high fever, so I went to bed early. They managed to put some sort of dinner on the table and had a great time together. After checking on me, Gifford announced that they were going for a ride. Off they went. At about ten o'clock, they returned home, excited. The three girls bounded into my room, Gifford tagging behind. In unison they announced, "Daddy bought a new car, Mother."

I sat up in bed. "A what?" I thought they were joking, but it was no joke.

All four of them tried to tell the story at the same time. They had started out on a drive and "just happened" to drive by the lot where a new station wagon was parked in all its shiny, aqua beauty! Dad and the girls decided to stop and look at it, and their enthusiasm encouraged him to give into the temptation of the moment. He agreed to buy it.

I didn't know how to react because I was crushed at the suddenness of his decision. To my knowledge, it was the first time in our married life that Gifford had ever done anything major without consulting me and without first praying about it with me. I was hurt.

Frankly, I was not too disappointed that he had decided against the camp. I had been privately struggling with feelings against the responsibility of beginning such a big project. Financing and directing a youth camp, as well as knowing that I would be responsible to manage the kitchen loomed like a giant task before me. I actually felt relieved that the camp was no longer a possibility.

We settled in for the night without our usual time of

prayer together, but neither of us slept much, which was unusual for Gifford. In the morning, his first statement to me was, "Honey, I've got to cancel that car." He had decided during the night. When I questioned him about the deposit he had paid, he replied that they could keep the money. The peace of heart he experienced when he made the decision to cancel the order was worth far more then the money he had paid down. The girls were disappointed when he told them that he was going to the bank to deposit the money for the camp instead of buying a new car but they lived through it.

Within a matter of days, we purchased the land, and negotiations to build Ikaho Bible Camp began. Literally thousands of young people attended the camps during the following twenty years, and it is impossible to estimate how many were born into the family of God as a result of their experience there. Many were drawn to a closer walk with the Lord, and marriages even resulted among the dedicated young people who worked together there. Our girls also enjoyed many summer months there, participating in camp life.

Two years after opening the camp, we were able to purchase the exact model station wagon that Gifford had chosen before, and did so for an unbelievably low price. It was even the same aqua color!

If Gifford had made a selfish decision and kept the first car, years of happy, fruitful ministry would have been lost. It is food for thought that within a matter of hours a person can make a decision that will influence one's whole lifetime and, as in this case, many other lives as well.

If we could communicate with Gifford today and ask him if he ever regretted buying the camp instead of the car, what do you think his answer would be?

9

BITTEN AGAIN

I left the house feeling great. I was happy! At long last I had everything in hand. The one little corner of my property that had been such a problem was to be settled, or so I thought. I walked confidently into the office that had been handling my legal affairs.

But my confidence was short-lived. One of my daughters had failed to answer one question on the forms I had sent to her, so the documents would have to be sent to America again, which would mean another long trip to the consulate for her and more weeks of delay for me.

It really wasn't the snag we had run into that irritated me the most. It was the lack of understanding and the arrogant attitude of the woman who processed the papers. My stomach muscles tightened as I found myself becoming angry. Knowing that I was about to say something I would regret later, I quickly excused myself. I was ashamed of my reaction, but the only thing I could do until I could control myself was to walk out of the office. Taking a new form, I mumbled something about having other business to attend to and said that I would return for more details later.

I went back to my car, overcome by remorse and disappointment in myself, surprised that I could become that angry at such a small offense after walking with Christ for nearly fifty years. Helpless to quiet the strong feelings, I wondered how my temper, although not expressed to anyone, could get the upper hand so quickly. I should never have reacted so strongly to another person's attitude.

When writing of this experience, I thought of the question Gifford once asked me when I expressed defeat in being disappointed in myself. "Why are you surprised at yourself?" he reminded me. "Didn't you know that's why you needed a Saviour in the first place?"

As I sat in the car, waiting for the turmoil in my heart to subside, the Lord brought to mind a Bible study I had taught the previous Friday morning. We had been studying John 3 and had looked particularly at verse 14, in which Jesus refers to the Old Testament story of the brass serpent (see Numbers 21:5-9). Christ said that He would be raised up on the cross in the same way that Moses had raised up the serpent. We had emphasized, as the context indicates, that Christ had original salvation from sin in mind, but we had concluded our discussion with the thought that poisonous snakes often attack even after salvation.

In the class, we talked about the symbolic poisonous snakes in our lives and gave them such names as "jealousy," "bitterness," "temper," and "greed." One sister brought to our attention that some of the Israelites had been on the journey a long time—ever since they had been freed from Egypt —yet they were bitten, too. In the car, this truth came to mind as I was reminded that my old sinful nature was as capable of being stirred to anger after forty-eight years as it was at the beginning of my walk with Christ.

Suddenly, there in the car, I saw myself as having been bitten again by one of the serpents of the Evil One, and the poison had brought the sin of anger into my life. At the same time, I remembered Numbers 21:9: *"If a serpent had bitten any man, when he beheld the serpent of brass, he lived."* In the class we had stressed that it only took a look at the serpent to bring instantaneous healing.

When I looked at the cross of Christ—my brass Serpent—I was instantly healed. The solution was that simple. I didn't need to run to a doctor to have the poison drained out. I didn't even need binding with a tourniquet to keep the poison from spreading anymore than it had. All I needed to do was take a quick, trustful glance at Christ in order to receive immediate spiritual healing. That's all that was necessary.

To this day, I can feel the thrill of the moment when I actually felt God relax my stomach muscles in answer to my simple prayer, "Lord," I prayed, "I've been bitten again. I'm sick. Please heal me." I immediately wanted to return to that office and face the woman again, but I was at a loss to explain to her how I had been able to complete my "other business" so quickly. My business with God had only taken a few seconds.

I can't help but contrast my experience that day with the many hours I have wasted under similar circumstances. Moping and pouting, feeling miserable and guilty, I have nursed my hurts instead of remembering this precious message: *"The preaching of the cross...unto us which are saved...is the power of God"* (1 Cor. 1:18). It takes only a look at the cross of Christ to receive the power of God in instantaneous forgiveness and healing.

I'm sure this is the thought Jeremiah had in mind when he wrote, *"Behold, I will send serpents...and they shall bite you, saith the Lord. Is not the Lord in Zion?...Is there no balm in Gilead; is there no physician there? Why, then is not the health of the daughter of my people recovered?"* (Jer. 8:17, 19, 22). Thank God there *is* balm in Gilead and there is a Physician. What a Saviour! What a message!

10
BRUISED REEDS

Have you ever felt like an isolated reed that has been out in the storm all night, battered about until you can't even lift your head? Have you ever felt absolutely worthless to yourself and to everyone else? Even worse, have you ever felt useless to God? Have you experienced jealousy when you are with people who never seem to suffer from indecision and inadequacy? Do you envy people who always know the right things to say and do? Do you feel at times that you are not living up to God's standards and are disappointing Him? If so, you'll understand how I felt one morning when I was struggling with these emotions.

Within and without, strong winds of adversity had joined together in pointing out my failures and shortcomings. I was shredded to pieces. Through accusations, Satan had succeeded in laying a colossal guilt trip on me for various failures as a missionary, a wife, and a mother. I picked up my Bible for comfort, and as I read Isaiah 42, I especially noticed the third verse. The Holy Spirit emphasized, *"A bruised reed shall He not break, and the smoking flax shall He not quench."*

I saw myself as that bruised reed and flickering wick. At the same time, Christ, by His Spirit, promised me personally that He would never snap me off and throw me away. Nor would He ever snuff out my tiny, smelly flame—never, no, never. He reminded me that He was bruised not only for all my sins, but for all my shortcomings and failures as well.

Christ assured me that my family and all the Japanese believers were included, since they were His responsibility. I honestly don't know what the outcome might have been had I not found His perfect peace, comfort, and hope by believing that He would remain true to His promise. He soon backed up these thoughts with 1 Corinthians 1:30, *"But of Him are ye in Christ Jesus, who of God is made unto us wisdom, and righteousness, and sanctification, and redemption."* It was as if He said to me, "How foolish of you to feel this way when I paid such a price to clear you of all that." For the next few days, I constantly claimed Him as my wisdom and righteousness, my sanctification and redemption. The bruises He received on the cross and His current high priestly work provided and continues to provide ample grace, far exceeding my needs.

In nature, there are numerous causes of bruising: wind, heavy rain, hail, snow, and human carelessness. This is also true of human reeds. We are easily damaged and the causes are many. Job, for instance, is a perfect example of a hopelessly battered reed. Circumstances, acts of nature, and his own wife all joined forces against him. Then, when his special friends came to "sympathize" with him, he became full of self-pity and cursed the day he was born. Later, because of their unjust accusations, he became defensive. He was a bruised reed, standing alone against the world. There are pat formulas by the dozens for straightening bruised reeds, but that morning and countless times since then, I discovered that God alone strengthens His reeds and He does so through His Word. Recognizing God's sovereignty, power, and love caused me to turn to Him for mercy and I was able to hold my head up again.

David too, realized that his answer lay in God. He said, *"Thou, O Lord, art a shield for me; my glory, and the lifter up of my head"* (Ps. 3:3). Not wallowing in self-condemnation or pity, he sent roots downward and kept himself in the sunshine of God's love. Fully believing God's promises gave him the strength from within to lift up his head. We, too, will be able to hold our heads high for His glory if we do the same.

11

BUSINESSWOMAN

We hear much these days about equal rights, equal pay, and equal benefits for women in the business world. The business world which swirls around us is real to us because we experience it daily. Nevertheless, there is another business, every bit as real. Because we cannot see it with our physical eyes we often are not conscious of it, but we should be. It is the spiritual business world, in which God gives women equal opportunity to prove their ability to do business for Him. Although the job assignments for women may differ from those of their brethren, God certainly provides equal pay and equal benefits of lasting, eternal value.

Christ gives examples of good and bad business deals. In Luke 19:12-27, He tells us about a prince who took a trip, leaving money in the hands of his servants to be used for trading: *"And it came to pass, that when he was returned, having received the kingdom, then he commanded these servants to be called unto him, to whom he had given the money, that he might know how much every man had gained by trading"* (Luke 19:15). We see, as we read this parable, that some servants used their talents wisely and were rewarded well. Others were not businesslike and gained little. One foolish man buried his share, so he received nothing.

It is impossible for us to know exactly what type of business the Lord had in mind when He told this story, but we can still draw parallels between spiritual and material business transactions. In the same way that we trade our time to a firm in exchange for a salary and the firm in turn trades its goods or services for money, we can trade our time for an "eternal" wage. By being creative, we should be able to come up with ways in which we can exchange this world's material goods and time for heaven's eternal currency.

During my early teen years, this thought was suggested to me. I remember, to this day, the joy I felt after giving my first gift to a missionary couple. I knew that the amount, as small as it was, had been credited to my heavenly bank account. I must confess it gives me another thrill, in remembering this incident, to realize that it has accumulated a great deal of interest in the intervening years!

In his message to the church in Laodicea, John records that the Lord counseled them *"to buy of Me gold tried in the fire, that thou mayest be rich; and white raiment, that thou mayest be clothed, and that the shame of thy nakedness do not appear; and anoint thine eyes with eye salve, that thou mayest see"* (Rev. 3:18).

Thinking of buying gold, I am reminded of an experience Gifford and I had prior to being evacuated from China in 1949. We were given three days' notice, during which time we had to sell our possessions and pack for immediate departure. We didn't have too many problems selling our belongings, but one big problem remained. Inflation had made Chinese currency practically worthless, and the money we received from our goods filled an entire room. Even if we had been able to ship the money, it would be of no value in the country to which we were going. The only solution was to exchange the money for something that had value that we could carry out with us.

Gifford found a money exchanger who was willing to exchange the large pile of currency for two tiny gold bars the size of the fingernail on my little finger. We put those bars in the arches of our shoes and walked out of China on the equivalent of a household of furnishings. Likewise, if we are to exchange our worldly possessions for heavenly gold, we must do it before we leave this world.

One great hindrance to our being diligent employees for God is caused by developing an attitude similar to the one the servant in Christ's parable had. Believing that his master was out for his own personal gain, he doubted his master's kindness and justice. This, in turn, caused fear and an unwillingness to trade the money that had been given to him. If we are not careful, a wrong perception of God will prevent us from trading temporal goods for eternal wealth.

The fact that God gave men and women equal time and talents should in itself be a challenge to us. Women will also be required to stand individually before our blessed Lord when He returns to take up His reign as King. Women, too, will be asked to give an account of their time and effort.

Let me share an example of a dear homemaker who, I believe, became a good spiritual businesswoman. She wanted to spread the gospel but couldn't do so because her husband, who was not a believer, limited her. One day, she heard that an evangelist needed a tape recorder for the Lord's work. The Lord laid it on her heart to begin praying for money to buy the recorder for him. She began to ask the Lord earnestly for a specific amount, but had no idea how God would answer her prayer.

One Saturday morning, her husband was asked to help a friend with a "do-it-yourself" plumbing job. Her husband knew she was disappointed because they had other plans, but she didn't voice any objections. When her husband returned home that evening, he handed her the exact amount of money she had been praying for with the explanation, "My friend gave me half of the money he saved by doing the job himself. Now I want to give my share to you."

This dear sister was surprised by her husband's action, but her husband was even more surprised when he saw the tears of joy his gift produced. Although puzzled, he was pleased when she explained how she had prayed for the money and how thrilled she was to receive it. The Lord rewarded her faithful work in prayer, and He will reward her again when she gets to heaven. Believe me, God will commend her for her good investment as He returns to her: "*...good measure, pressed down, and shaken together, and running over...*" (Luke 6:38).

12
CONTENTMENT

Elisha and his servant were staying with a Shunammite woman and her husband, enjoying wonderful hospitality in the comfortable room the couple had just added to their home for the express purpose of entertaining the Lord's servants. In return for their generous care, Elisha asked her what she would like to receive from the Lord as a reward, assuring her that God would grant any request she made (2 Kings 4:8-37). She could ask for new opportunities, a change in her circumstances, material possessions, or anything else she longed for, and God would give it to her. My, wouldn't I be thrilled with such an offer!

But her answer was surprising. She asked for none of these things. She simply answered, *"I dwell among mine own people."* In other words, she told the prophet that she was content with her circumstances just as they were and needed nothing. Actually, it was Elisha's servant who, noticing there were no children in the home, suggested that on her behalf they ask the Lord to give her a child. God granted the request and gave her a special baby, but a few years later, the child took sick and died within a day. Even in the face of this great loss, we see her maintaining the same quiet peace and assurance, expressing contentment and trust with the words, *"It shall be well."*

The woman laid the boy's body on Elisha's bed, closed the door, and walked out to find Elisha, apparently having complete trust that God would resurrect the boy. Before she became pregnant, she was contented. After the Lord took her child, she was still content to leave the circumstances in God's hands. In the natural way of responding to situations, it couldn't have been all right with her that her son died. Nor was it easy for her to shut the door on her problem and walk away. Yet she had such intimacy with the Lord that she fully trusted Him even though He took away what He had given. We would all find it advantageous to accept His will and say from our hearts, "It is well!" no matter what circumstances we find ourselves in. As this story unfolds, we learn that God did raise her son from the dead in response to her faithful and accepting attitude.

Paul gives us an interesting thought in 1 Timothy 6:6, *"Godliness with contentment is great gain."* Godliness must be accompanied by contentment to be fully effective. Many of us continually strive to be more like our Saviour, but at times we allow ourselves to be dissatisfied with situations in life. If we listened to our own conversations for ten minutes, we would realize that God needs to teach us to be content with our families, our homes, our local churches, our Christian leaders, and the world in general. To me, contentment is the equivalent of what the author meant when he wrote, *"For we which have believed do enter into rest"* (Heb. 4:3). Contentment is a state of the soul, and we receive discernment through the Word of God to recognize the difference between what we only want for ourselves and what we really desire for God's glory.

Our most effective weapon against dissatisfaction is the Word of God: *"For the Word of God is quick, and powerful, and sharper than any two-edged sword, piercing even to the dividing asunder of soul and spirit, and of the joints and marrow, and is a discerner of the thoughts and intents of the heart"* (Heb. 4:12). If we have His discernment, we will be both godly and content.

When we learn to rest in God, we are content. Restlessness and dissatisfaction usually come when we rebel against God because we feel He has let us down. When we verbalize our discontentment to others, we are, in effect, saying to the world that our God has given us a bad deal and that we deserve to have a much better lot in life. Much reproach is brought to the Lord by disgruntled Christians.

It's impossible for us to be content with every detail in the lives of our spouses, our children, our jobs, or in the community around us, but we can have inner peace, resting in the knowledge that Almighty God is in control. I'm looking forward to meeting this dear, contented, Shunammite woman in heaven and telling her what an example she has been to me by challenging me to work toward genuine contentment. True contentment comes by laying the problem down, shutting the door on the problem, and making my way to Him.

13
DID MARTHA LEARN HER LESSON?

I think of Martha as an efficient, hospitable lady. All three times we read about her in Scripture, we find her surrounded by people. Twice she is pictured as a hostess entertaining many guests. No doubt she was the type of person who makes herself welcome in any community because she is always serving someone.

The Lord was welcome in Martha's home at any time, and He had a special place in His heart for both her and her sister, Mary. However, even though she had many good characteristics, Martha had at least one weak point. When she was under strain, she criticized people. We find the Lord correcting her for this fault the first time we are introduced to her in Luke 10:38-42.

If John hadn't especially mentioned in his book that Jesus loved Martha (Jn. 11:5), I might have thought that the Lord was a bit hard on her, perhaps even a little tactless. He made her fault known by rebuking her in front of her guests. We read that she had complained to the Lord about Mary's inactivity, but instead of giving her the sympathy she was expecting, He praised Mary. Martha could easily have been deeply hurt and humiliated by this. I empathize with Martha because I don't like to be corrected in private, much less in front of others.

The Lord didn't let her give in to her self-pity, however. He told her that her attitude was wrong and that Mary was right in desiring to fellowship with Him. He wanted to teach Martha the importance of right perspectives.

The Scriptures are often short on details, but by using my imagination and reading a little between the lines, I believe a great change took place within Martha after this incident. Soon afterward, we see her back at the kitchen stove serving again. This time she is not grumbling or complaining, despite the fact that she had even greater reason to complain because Mary is giving Christ not only her time but an expensive gift as well. I think it is noteworthy that Martha did not become weary or give up in service because Christ rebuked her. I believe that Martha had learned her lesson.

Martha accepted the chastisement of the Lord graciously and profited from it. When I think of Martha, I think of James 1:12, *"Blessed is the man that endureth temptation: for when he is tried, he shall receive the crown of life, which the Lord hath promised to them that love Him."* I believe the crown of life is the reward given to people who learn to endure for Christ's sake. It's a crown given to people who are faithful to Christ in all circumstances by submitting willingly and running the race right to the finish line.

Martha endured open rebuke and matured spiritually because she graciously received correction. Thinking of Martha in this way has renewed my desire to receive the crown of life. I want the sheer delight of having at least this one crown to place at His feet as I join the heavenly hosts in saying, *"Thou are worthy, O Lord, to receive glory and honor..."* (Rev. 4:11).

14
DINAH—A RESTLESS YOUNG LADY

Dinah, the daughter of Jacob and Leah, woke up one morning with an unusually restless spirit—triggered, perhaps, by inactivity. Genesis 34:1-3 simply says that she left the house to make friends with neighboring women. She suddenly was overcome by a desire to see how the rest of the world lived. Actually, there is nothing wrong with such a desire. It is very normal for a young person to want to make new friends, but Dinah had been taught specifically that God demanded separation from the heathen people around them because they did not believe in or follow the one, true, Living God of Israel.

Sympathizing with her boredom of everyday life, we understand the frame of mind with which she more than likely left home that morning. No doubt she felt like an oddball in a strange land. This feeling is a common reaction of children who are raised in a godly environment, even today. We can also identify with her reactions when a charming, smartly dressed young man approached her and started a conversation. I can see her eyes light up as he aroused her interest. She was elated to learn that he was the Hivite prince of the land—a fact which flattered her ego. As they talked further, she was attracted to him in response to his interest in her.

One step led to another until, as it tells us in Scripture, *"he took her, and lay with her, and defiled her. And his soul clave unto Dinah"* (Gen. 34:23). What had started innocently went from bad to worse, bringing devastating results. As a consequence of her restlessness, she found herself at the point of no return.

This could not have happened if she had stayed among her own people. (This, of course, is not true in isolated cases of rape.) Disgrace fell on her family. In response, her people retaliated against the Hivites, killing every male. The very people she went out to meet were slaughtered for one sexual act.

Another sobering story recorded in 2 Samuel 11 proves that big things grow from small beginnings which are often the result of a restless spirit. From King David's vantage point on the palace roof, he saw Bathsheba bathing in the privacy of her courtyard on the roof and invited her to the palace. We are all well acquainted with the story. Bathsheba no doubt responded to his invitation innocently, but she soon permitted herself to be placed in a situation where intimacy was expressed. The fourth verse says that "She came to him," which suggests that she went to him voluntarily in response to his invitation. If she had limited the opportunity to express their passionate emotions before they became involved, it would have been comparatively easy to squelch such unholy desire.

In the case of David and Bathsheba, the thought of another person had broken into the sanctity of marriage, as it does in many marriages today. It was not nipped in the bud, so it took preeminence and robbed their home of true love, peace, and joy. As Christian women, we are responsible to guard ourselves against being tempted or becoming a temptation to others. We cannot permit anything to take our thoughts away from our responsibilities. This principle is also true of women who are single.

Not too long ago, I had a sad conversation with a dear sister. She told me how the breakdown in her spiritual life began with only a few twinges of dissatisfaction in her marital circumstances. These soon grew into a critical spirit, which drove her to seek new male friendships. With bitter tears of remorse, she shared details of the results of her actions. Although she has the assurance of God's forgiveness, she will continue to bear the consequences of her sin for the rest of her life. She permitted an evil thought to grow in the recesses of her mind and it later blossomed, bringing a harvest of noxious fruit.

God, knowing the possibilities of the mind for evil, commanded that we keep busy by diligent work. We have often heard that an idle mind is a good workshop for the devil. God will spare us from struggling with evil memories, suffering through hours of self-condemnation and regrets, and reliving unpleasant experiences if we cooperate with Him. It pays to keep short accounts with God by bringing our minds into captivity to Jesus Christ. Much of the evil in personal lives, family breakdowns, and in the church today begins with a mere twinge of boredom, restlessness, or a disgruntled spirit.

15
DISAPPOINTMENTS

If you had told me years ago that I would awaken one day and actually be able to praise the Lord for disappointments, I would have emphatically retorted, "No way!" My disappointments were too real and too painful at the time, but that actually happened this morning.

Awakening early, I thought back to my late teenage years, which were pretty miserable. My father had moved our family from a thriving, happy church with a lively young people's group of seventy-some members in order to help a small, struggling church in a farming community with few young people. I needed to make all new friends, and the nearest potential girlfriend was a two-mile walk from our house. While making the adjustment, I thought I would die of loneliness.

In order to escape that feeling, I would shut myself in the empty church building and practice the piano for hours. Those lonely feelings came back this morning as I pictured myself in the front of the building, at the piano, glancing back at the closed doors in hopes that a certain "Prince Charming" would suddenly make a dashing appearance and whisk me away for a date. But alas, that never happened. The one tall, dark, and handsome eligible bachelor had all the young ladies in the community wishing the same thing. I didn't stand a chance.

After one such long afternoon, in bitter disappointment I told my mother, "I wish I had never been born. I have absolutely nothing to live for." I meant every word of it. As that scene unfolded before me this morning, I thanked God that the particular Prince Charming did not come. Although a professing Christian, he would not have influenced my life for good the way that my husband, Gifford, had done.

Thinking back to those years, I remember that because of sheer boredom I began to accompany my father to other small churches in order to play the piano when no one else could play. During the long rides going and coming, my father and I built a special relationship that lasted until the Lord took him home. We memorized Scripture together and he taught me many of life's real values. For example, he often told me what to expect in the man I would eventually marry. This morning, for the first time, I linked piano playing to my real Prince Charming, whom I met while playing the piano in a servicemen's center in Saint Petersburg, Florida. I thanked God once again from the bottom of my heart that God had kept me for Gifford.

This morning, after hundreds of disappointments, I lay in bed waiting for dawn to break and thanked God for many similar things that I had so desperately wanted to happen but which never did. The flashbacks poured in until they were mountain-sized. Memories of delays, thwarted plans and dreams, people who had let me down, lonely hours, and even dozens of seemingly unanswered prayers became the object of thanksgiving.

One memory in particular was of a morning when we awoke to find that the nightmare of the previous evening had actually become a reality. The missionary work of fifteen years lay shattered at our feet. But I could see that God used these experiences to teach me. Looking back, I realized that He arranged things in ways which had actually worked for the best for all concerned.

I'm sure Martha and Mary were disappointed when they thought Christ had let them down, too. They watched their brother, Lazarus, deteriorate and die. Their disappointment increased hourly. It would have helped just to know that the

Lord was aware of their suffering. Instead, He chose to stay away in silence. He let them handle all the preparations and hold the funeral without one expression of comfort from Him, because He did not arrive in time to do anything for their brother who died.

When Christ said to Martha, *"I am the resurrection, and the life,"* He was drawing attention to Himself as the source of life itself. He was saying, "Martha, I am Lord." I believe He was deliberately linking Himself, the Messiah, to the God of the Old Testament Who had said, *"I kill and I make alive; I wound, and I heal"* (Deut. 32:39).

This morning, I realized that Christ takes full responsibility for all of my disappointments and delays, too. They are only one of His methods of wounding. I began to thank the Lord for each memory that came, one by one. It wasn't long before I knew that a strange thing was happening. Ill feelings I had harbored against certain people for years began to melt away, and healing came from inside. His healing balm continuously poured into my soul as I praised Him.

If I had only believed God and trusted Him more during the various wounding and healing processes of my life, I would have been healed much sooner. Instead, I actually picked at the sores by hashing over wrongs and thus hindered my healing.

I thought that what I wanted would make me happier than what He planned for me. I had thought that my ways of getting satisfaction were better than His. I was actually putting my ideas above the Lord's. With this attitude, it was no wonder that I became bitterly disillusioned time and time again.

While writing this chapter about delays and disappointments, a lesson from God's nature unfolded before my eyes. A crabapple tree I could see from my kitchen window—which had looked dead all winter—was springing to life. The buds that I would have ruined if I had attempted to open them prematurely with my clumsy fingers were beginning to blossom and display their full color. If in this life, I don't see my dreams and hopes mature, I know with assurance that God will *"...give...beauty for ashes, the oil of joy for mourning, the garment of praise for the spirit of heaviness...that He might be glorified"* (Isa. 61:3).

It has taken me years to finally agree that the situations that turned out best were the situations I let Him work out on my behalf. No doubt that, if I believe that He loves me and let Him work out His plans for my life, I will face far fewer disappointments and will be better able to handle the ones that do come. One thought brought special thanksgiving: I contemplated the awfulness of an eternity of God's silence. He may be silent for short periods of discipline and training now, but it's only to prepare me better for eternal fellowship.

16
ESTHER, A KERNEL OF WHEAT

God's name is not mentioned in the Book of Esther (some have suggested it is hidden four times in acrostic form), yet God is very much at work in the lives of His people throughout the book, especially in the lives of Esther and her cousin, Mordecai.

Esther's husband—the King of Persia—made a proclamation that would destroy the Jewish race while under the influence of one of his high administrative officials, Haman. King Ahasuerus, who did not know his beautiful queen was an Israelite, was caught unaware in the trap of being party to a plan of genocide.

It's not too hard for us to imagine Esther's terrific struggle, created by the news of the diabolical scheme her husband had agreed to concerning the Jewish race. Mordecai advised her to go to the king and to plead with him on Israel's behalf. But this created a problem for her. Although she was married to the king, she did not have the right to speak freely. She did not have the liberty to ask for an audience with the king. But Mordecai insisted she must do this if she was to save the Jewish people.

Esther and Mordecai decided between themselves to spend three days in fasting (is prayer implied?) before she approached the king. Those three days must have been pure torture. Esther knew well that the king had dealt harshly with Vashti, his former queen, and that she risked everything if she went into his presence uninvited. She was also tempted not to reveal her Jewish identity, hoping that if she did nothing the king would not discover her nationality and thus she would be saved. She knew the truth, however, that it was more then likely that he would find out anyway. Neither alternative was acceptable to her; her heart was torn in two.

I don't think that Esther tried to manipulate God during the three days she spent in fasting. I view it as a time when she brought her stormy will into subjection to God's will. Mustering up courage and conquering her fear, she gained the strength to be able to do as she had said to Mordecai, *"If I perish, I perish"* (Esther 4:16). During this agony of spirit, Esther became brave enough to make the ultimate sacrifice: to risk her life to save her people according to the will of God.

With a pounding heart, she walked into the court of the king, but armed with preparation of heart from her days of soul preparation. When the king saw her, she found favor with him. He held out his golden scepter to her and promised her even half of his kingdom. God honored the faith of this wise, contemplative woman and gave her step-by-step plans during the following few days. She proceeded slowly and deliberately under God's guidance.

What follows is extremely interesting. The king not only considered her request but, under the tutelage of Mordecai, created a new law. This law superseded the first law, giving the Jews the right to fight back against any armed forces that might attack them and even the right to take the property of the enemy as spoil.

Esther had not heard Christ say, *"Whosoever shall lose his life for My sake...shall save it"* (Mark 8:35). Nor had she heard Him declare, *"Except a corn of wheat fall into the ground and die, it abides alone: but if it die, it bringeth forth much fruit"* (John 12:24). Nevertheless, she knew and practiced the principle found in both of these passages. In doing so, she became a living example of Romans 12:1-2. By making the decision to stand before the king, she presented her body a living sacrifice to God.

As a result of her sacrifice, Esther proved that God's will was good, acceptable, and perfect. She had the joy of watching Him take all the details, fit them into place, and accomplish truly great things. Her life was spared, her family was saved, and the whole nation of Israel was given the opportunity to fight to preserve itself from annihilation. In addition to those amazing accomplishments, many Gentiles began to fear the Lord and chose to join the people of God. Esther's personal sacrifice in being willing to die changed the history of the world. Later, the preserved nation of Israel produced the Saviour, God's Messiah. These far-reaching results are felt even to our present day, and we know that God has still not finished working out His purpose for the Jewish race.

17

EVERY WISE WOMAN

"*Every wise woman buildeth her house: but the foolish plucketh it down with her hands*" (Prov. 14:1). When I read this verse, Christ's words in Matthew 7 flashed into my mind: "*Whosoever heareth these sayings of Mine, and doeth them, I will liken him unto a wise [wo]man who built his [her] house upon a rock: and the rain descended, and the floods came, and the winds blew, and beat upon that house,; and it fell not: for it was founded upon a rock.*"

Only the wise woman who builds her personal life on the Rock—Christ Jesus—will build her house wisely. She must make a lifetime commitment to hear His words and to do them. If she doesn't, bitterness, unbelief, injured pride, resentment, or an unforgiving spirit will pluck down what she has built. This can happen at any stage of building a home.

One lovely example of wisely building such a home is Naomi, who did not have a particularly wise start. During one period, her home was plucked down. In unbelief, she and her husband fled from the Promised Land into Moab to avoid the difficulties of a famine. This was not only a foolish move but evidence of a lack of faith. They did not believe that God was able to provide as He had promised.

However, after God took her husband and two sons, Naomi developed a great longing to return to God and His people. Naomi's faith, instead of being lessened, increased through her tragic experiences. It did not crumble even after three consecutive deaths in the family. Cold rains of trouble descended; floods of adversity rose. The winds of trial were strong, but her spiritual foundation grew stronger.

I'm sure that the thoughts of returning to her old friends and family were not pleasant. She had been stripped of all she had previously taken pride in. She most certainly knew she would face the I-told-you-so attitude of pious Jews who weathered the famine. Also there would be disapproving glances from the Jewish community toward her Gentile daughter-in-law. Naomi let none of these fears deter her. She was determined to give up the past to begin life again.

However, Naomi nearly forfeited this opportunity when she suggested that her daughters-in-law return to their un-saved families and heathen gods solely because their chances to remarry would be slim in her homeland. Instead, Naomi exemplified Proverbs 28:13, *"He that covereth his sins shall not prosper: but whoso confesseth and forsaketh them shall have mercy."* She recognized her wrong and decided to go back to seek her God. Forsaking the life she had established in Moab, she turned her face in determination toward Bethlehem.

Once she made the choice to go back to the Promised Land, her daughter-in-law, Ruth, decided to go back with her (Ruth 1). God rewarded Naomi's principles of godliness and proved to her that He was able to make all grace abound to-ward her. He gave her the joy of building her house again in middle age by giving her another son-in-law, Boaz. Through this marriage between Ruth and Boaz, she was given a grand-child and her good influence was felt on him. To her last days, Naomi was able to build such an unusual household through Ruth and Boaz that its record still stands today.

We, too, should be encouraged to build our homes into old age, believing that God is bigger than any of our sins or fool-ish mistakes that for a time might pluck down what we have built. Through humility, faithfulness, and confession of sin, God will give us another chance if we build upon the Rock. He will enable us to succeed in building our homes, knowing our labor is never in vain. Christ says, *"Be thou faithful unto death, and I will give thee a crown of life"* (Rev. 2:10).

18
FROM AN OLDER SISTER

Having been asked, as an older sister, to pass on simple advice to the younger sisters in the family of God, I sat down to write an article using Titus 2:3-5:

The aged women likewise, that they be in behavior as becometh holiness, not false accusers, not given to much wine, teachers of good things; that they may teach the young women to be sober, to love their husbands, to love their children, to be discreet, chaste, keepers at home, good, obedient to their own husbands, that the Word of God be not blasphemed.

As I read this passage, I was awestruck at the position older women play in God's program for His Church. It is a big order that the teaching by older women must always be preceded by and accompanied by holy living. For example, I must be an example before I qualify to teach others. A Christian woman never reaches the age of retirement when she no longer needs to teach through the example of her godly life.

Thinking about my own responsibility as an older woman, I couldn't get past verse three: *"The aged women likewise, that they be in behavior as becometh holiness."* If I fail to conduct myself as an example of holiness, I can still be an example in humbleness by admitting my failure, apologizing, and making things right. Christ is building His Church out of ordinary people like you and me.

How can I teach younger women to be sober-minded if I am a frivolous older sister? How can I teach them to love if I'm an angry old lady? There is no power in instructing them to be discreet if I am not discerning and do not show good judgment. Nor can I teach them to be chaste if impure thoughts penetrate my mind. This same principle is true of keeping the home and of being good and obedient. If I don't conquer and obtain victory over these things daily in my life, how can I help my younger sisters know how to live out the teaching of Titus 2?

In Titus 2:3, Paul says that older women, especially, are not to be false accusers. Here I make a distinction between "not false" and "not accusers." This phrase reminds me of an incident that took place early in my missionary life. I was spouting off to my husband about what I thought a certain Christian was doing wrong. Gifford turned to me and asked if I actually knew whether what I was saying was the truth. "Have you gotten it secondhand," he asked, "or, even worse, is it just suspicion?" I had to admit that I learned the information secondhand. He then added, "Honey, please be careful what you pass on to me because what you say influences my thoughts about that person." From that day on, I have tried to guard against becoming a gossipy woman. More than one church has been torn apart through false accusations or because people pass on others' weaknesses and failures.

Paul continues, "...*not given to much wine.*" I don't think wine is really a problem with many older sisters at my local church, but it is good to think of this because our lives should not center around temporal things that provide enjoyment. We should never allow the "here and now" to cause us to forget the eternal, nor let it take control of us by indulgence. I'm sure that if I were more aware of eternity, I would find it easier to sort out my priorities, remembering that I can never retire as a role model to younger sisters.

My advice to my younger sisters in the Lord is that to become older women who are useful in teaching others in the Church of God, they will have to begin at whatever age they are now. We do not become godly older sisters without cultivating Christian virtues in our younger years. Through practice, those virtues will increase with age.

Besides being role models before people, we Christians—young and old, men and women—do well to remember that the spirit world is watching us. Paul tells us in Ephesians 3:10, *"To the intent that now unto the principalities and powers in heavenly places might be known by the church the manifold wisdom of God."* It is a far-reaching truth that what I do, how I react, and what I say are not only observed by people around us but by the spirit world. It is easy to forget that spirits are real and that they watch our private, public, and church life.

It might be well to remember, too, that age is relative. There is always someone younger than me to teach. Recently, I heard about a single sister who has a special interest in the spiritual welfare of young people in our local assembly. She periodically takes one of them out for dinner with the express purpose of finding out his or her spiritual values and goals. She continually tries to encourage them toward greater spiritual growth.

It is my constant prayer that at the Judgment Seat of Christ, after the wood, hay, and stubble are burned and blown away from my life, that He will find a foundation in which precious stones are deeply imbedded that will sparkle through eternity for His glory.

19
GOD ALWAYS HAS SOMEONE

Have you ever noticed the number of times in Scripture that God prepared various things or people for special service to Himself, ahead of when that preparation would be needed? He created some things for a particular purpose, such as a fish, a gourd, a worm, and an east wind. (These examples are from the Book of Jonah; other examples exist elsewhere in Scripture). But I'm not thinking about fish and worms; rather, the special people God has used to fill the personal needs of the saints.

When I think back through the years, I am astounded by how often God prepared people to be there just when I needed them the most. God always has someone! This has been especially true since I became a widow, but I am getting ahead of myself. Allow me to tell some of our experiences when Gifford and I first arrived in China in 1947.

Gifford was delayed in Shanghai getting our baggage through customs, so we thought it would be wise for me to start ahead of him by ship up the Yangtze River. He would follow by plane. So we arranged to travel with a veteran missionary family to the port closest to their mission station. There, I would wait for Gifford to join me.

The first week of traveling went as planned, then our three-month-old baby, Ruth, got dysentery from the water and became very sick. By the time we arrived at the port, it seemed like all her intestines had been discharged. Her drastic weight loss made her look like a shriveled-up old lady, and I was very alarmed when I saw blood in her stools. We made it to the mission compound and the care of a missionary nurse, but it was evident we urgently needed to get her to a doctor. All the missionaries showed much concern and prayed a great deal for her.

Arrangements were immediately made for Ruth and me to fly to Chungking for medical help. Gifford was able to buy a ticket in Shanghai for the same plane. A coworker from our station agreed to meet us in Chungking and to serve as interpreter because I spoke no Chinese and Gifford had forgotten his. Reservations were made for us at the C.I.M. mission home. Everything possible had been thought of and worked out in detail—all but the weather, that is.

I met Gifford's plane at Nangking, and we boarded on schedule, feeling confident and relaxed since we were a family again and would soon have Ruth in the hands of a good doctor. The plane was a troop-transport; passengers were lined against the sides and baggage was tied to the floor in the center. We sure didn't have any comforts of modern air travel, but we were grateful to be on our way. It didn't even bother me that, apart from our own conversation, I never heard a single word of English during the whole trip because I felt assured that we would be met in Chungking.

Our first alarm came when we arrived at the airport and no foreigner met us as expected. Our second concern was that we had not touched down in the city of Chungking but rather on an island, where a wide river separated us from our destination. There had been no message of explanation from anyone, so by this time I was really uneasy. After a long wait, during which we did not understand what was going on, we noticed a ferry approaching from the other side of the river. When the other passengers boarded the ferry and someone motioned us to do the same, we followed suit, hoping we would still see an American's face at the other side.

Just before the ferry reached the dock, a well-dressed Chinese gentleman approached us and asked in perfect English,

"What is your baby's name?" He had understood our conversation on the plane and later at the airport. He had been aware of our consternation all along, but wasn't sure whether or not to offer help. He then assured us that if there was no one in Chungking to help us, he would hire a rickshaw to take us to the mission home. From our conversation, he knew we lacked the language to hire a rickshaw and could not give the rickshaw man directions or barter for the fare. He turned out to be very kind and friendly and was true to his word. Before we reached the shore, he had written directions in Chinese and had taken money from our hand in preparation to pay the rickshaw man. When the ferry arrived, he let the man know not to overcharge us. He was returning from the United States to inland China, but I firmly believe he was sent by God to be on our plane in order to save the life of our baby and to help two frantic parents. What perfect timing when we needed it most! I wanted so badly to hug him when we parted, but I didn't dare.

Soon after we arrived at the home, a message came from the missionary friend who had promised to meet us. He had been held up by a flood and couldn't cross the river until the water level came down. He had no idea how long he would have to wait before he could come. This delay turned out to be of the Lord because Ruth needed extra treatment. She was cared for by a missionary doctor who was an expert in dysentery-type diseases and happened to be staying in Chungking at the time. This was not chance either; it was a direct provision of the Lord. This doctor did not know about Ruth but was there when needed. By the time the missionary arrived to escort us to our mission station, Ruth was well on the way to recovery. She had responded very well to treatment in answer to the many prayers offered for her.

We had two-and-a-half happy years working in fellowship with the missionary family in Kweiyang, Kweichow. Those years created good memories. Then one day we received a letter from the American Embassy ordering us to leave China immediately because our city was completely surrounded by the Communist army. We were again on the move, flying to Hong Kong this time. We had planned to go directly to Japan but discovered in transit that we were not allowed to enter Japan with a baby under a year old because the living conditions were still so poor after the war. So we had to wait until our second daughter, Esther, was a year old.

Hong Kong was flooded with immigrants from all over China, so we decided it would be better to wait in Taiwan. We had no trouble renting a house in Taipei but were then faced with a new problem. After the expenses of traveling, paying a huge deposit on a house, and setting up housekeeping, our resources were greatly depleted. Our mail was not coming through because no one in the States had been able to keep up with our plans, which had changed so suddenly. We soon found ourselves in an extremely distressing and embarrassing situation.

Our electric bill had been delivered and we were not able to pay it. Gifford called to ask for an extension, but was refused. He was told that our electricity would be shut off the next day at noon. After the phone call and a good time of prayer, He and I decided to go for a walk, leaving our two children in the care of a single missionary. Not three blocks from home, we met a believer from the nearby assembly who was also trying to find relief from the intense summer heat during the cool of the evening. We had a nice time of fellowship as he joined us. When we parted, he pulled something from his pocket, saying that he had received a letter from a friend in America that day. His friend had enclosed a twenty-dollar bill, which he said was illegal for him to cash, so he slipped it into Gifford's hand, asking him to please cash it and use it.

This time I wanted to burst into tears, but again I restrained myself. We returned home with much praise and thanksgiving because the twenty dollars covered the electric bill and gave us a little extra besides.

Another crisis came a few years after Gifford passed away, when I was going through a difficult time spiritually and emotionally. That day I was at an all-day church gathering. About noon, I succumbed completely to a spirit that I knew was not from the Lord. I was so overcome with self-pity and discouragement that I had to leave the service to return home in defeat.

I had no more than walked through the door when the mailman arrived, delivering a big, fat letter from my sister. I didn't have much heart to read it, but I opened it anyway. It was full of love and warm, encouraging news about the whole family. She closed the letter by reconfirming her love for me and stressed the fact that everybody at home was praying for me. Deeply touched, in the privacy of my study I freely released the fountain of tears that had been building up all morning. After a time of prayer and confession, I felt much better. I confessed to the Lord that I had been consumed with self-pity and had forgotten His great love for me, which He clearly expressed through my sister. I felt so lighthearted that I returned to my Christian friends and enjoyed the rest of the day.

Whether I faced a language barrier, dire financial needs, or emotional and spiritual problems, I can say with assurance that God has always had someone to help me when I needed it. No less wonderful have been the countless times when a Christian brother has called to ask if I had any leaky faucets or problems with the car that he could help me with. This happened in Japan as well as since retiring to the United States. God has proven Himself through His people to be *"a very present help in trouble"* (Ps. 46:1).

20
GOD BLESSES A FAITHFUL NUISANCE

I awakened from my nap to the sound of weeping. The minute I walked into the living room and saw my dear friend, I knew something dreadful had happened because she was the first Japanese adult I'd seen cry. Their Buddhist culture trains them to suppress and eliminate expressions of emotion, but my friend cried unashamedly. I sat down beside her and tried to discover the source of such devastation.

When she regained enough control of herself to talk, she referred to herself as an "ojama mono," which means a nuisance or something in the way. Gradually she was able to tell me that she had been given three days to make a life-changing decision. If her answer was affirmative, she would become the wife of a widower and mother to his two young children. If it was negative, she would have to leave home and forfeit all the benefits of belonging to her family. They would then take no further responsibility for her even in sickness and death. I had heard bits and pieces of my friend's story before, but had never heard it all in detail until that afternoon. I'd like to share it with you.

Several years previously, my friend had been engaged to a young man she truly loved. Just before the wedding, her father was diagnosed with cancer and became terminally ill. Since she was a registered nurse and the only daughter not married, the family decided that she should postpone her marriage in order to care for her dying father. Her fiance' agreed to wait six months, but as her father lingered, he lost interest in her and married another woman a year later.

Disappointed at this change in her situation and also seeing her friends marry, have children, and live normal lives, caused her to become angry and bitter. It was bad enough to be brokenhearted, but to be left out of life's mainstream was even worse. After her father died, she became depressed and even attempted suicide. Then one day, she chanced upon a street meeting, stopped to listen, and heard the gospel for the first time. After the meeting, a Christian invited her to a cottage meeting. A few months later, she received Christ as her Saviour.

When she became a new creature in Christ Jesus, she was delivered from the power of darkness and became a citizen of the kingdom of God's dear Son. She found new meaning in life. Yet the difficulties of her life continued in spite of her change in heart and attitude.

Her major difficulty was that her elder brother lived in the family home with his growing family, as was the custom. His wife began to let her know that they needed more space, so it was time for her to marry and move out. They began treating her as an "ojama mono," and her marital status became the topic of conversation at all the family gatherings. She insisted that since she was now a Christian, she did not want to be unequally yoked with an unbeliever. Ignoring her protests, the family arranged one meeting after another with eligible bachelors. She had two marriage proposals, but she held onto her conviction that she could never be one with someone who held such different views of life and eternity.

Her family lost patience with her thinking, considering it to be nothing more than stubbornness and rebellion. So they decided to give her one last chance. They arranged a meeting with the recently widowed Buddhist priest of their village. When he showed interest in her, the family—especially her mother—thought they had made a perfect match by joining a deeply religious man with an equally religious woman. In order to put pressure on her, they came up with the ultimatum of her having to leave home if she did not agree to their marriage plans. They gave her a three-day deadline to make up her mind. She still did not capitulate, but burst into tears and walked out. Then she came over to us, leaving her surprised family behind.

This was our first encounter with the Japanese custom of arranged marriages, which seemed strange to us. We were sure the marriage would never work, but knew she had to decide herself. Many earnest prayers arose during the three days she stayed with us prior to making her decision. At one point, she raised the question of the proposal being from the Lord because it would give her the opportunity to raise the two children and bring them to Sunday School. She soon realized, however, the impossibility of a Buddhist priest consenting to that plan.

At one point, I saw that she was weakening, but after a time of prayer together I was amazed to see her tears stop flowing as soon as she made up her mind to follow the Lord at all costs. She would not compromise. She would trust Him for her future. The family, on hearing her decision, were true to their threat and asked her to leave the family home.

Then came the next big hurdle—finding her a place to live while she looked for new employment. She had been the village's respected midwife, but in her small farming community, she was ostracized because of her stand for Christ. The whole community took the side of her family. The family had lost face by her refusal to marry the revered priest, so she was no longer welcome at community social events.

It was a wonderful answer to prayer and a great relief when the Lord provided a good position as resident midwife in a private obstetric hospital near Tokyo. Her two most serious problems, employment and housing were solved at the same time. To cushion her time of adjustment, I made regular overnight trips to visit her. I have vivid memories of seeing her stand before an open window and watch school children pass in great numbers, and heard her earnestly pray that God would send someone to witness to them of Christ's love.

As a result of her faithful prayers and witness, during one of my visits the wife of one the leading doctors in the hospital was saved. Later this woman attended a church in Tokyo and asked a few of the Christians to begin a Bible study in her home. Her salvation was only the beginning. Through the years, the Lord has led three missionaries to settle in that area, and a thriving work has blossomed into a well-established church. I am convinced that when my friend stands before the Lord, and sees the fruit her decision produced and receives her crown of life, she will be able to say with hosts of others that the misunderstandings, loneliness, and heartaches were worth it all.

21
GOD'S EYES

During an illness in later life, my mother was resting with her eyes closed as she recovered from surgery. My brother and I had joined my sister at the hospital to provide comfort and keep Mother company, but she was too sick to notice us. Unable to muster enough strength to even answer our questions, she ignored us, which was unlike her normal behavior.

Since it was late in the evening, we moved into a corner of the room and talked in undertones so as not to disturb her roommate. The three of us discussed how unusual it was to see Mother's eyes be so unresponsive, not even seeming to be aware that we were in the room. The conversation went back to our childhood, and we reminisced about how much control she had had over all of her children through the different expressions in her eyes. We each had memories of incidents of mischief avoided and times when we were reprimanded by her gaze.

In bed that night, I thought more about Mother's unusually expressive, dark-brown eyes and remembered how many messages had been sent to me through them. (Much more would have been communicated had she always been able to catch my attention!) When I knew I needed her correction the most, I would hide behind something or someone to make sure she wasn't able to express her displeasure with me through her eyes.

I recalled times when she was teaching Sunday school or a youth class. Knowing that I was acting badly, I would duck behind a classmate when I wanted to send a note or whisper to a friend, but Mother had an uncanny intuition about what was going on and would soon align herself with me again so that she could catch my eye. Her nonverbal message came through clear and strong: "You'd better straighten up, and fast!"

I also remembered taking advantage of the situation while visitors were in our home. I would make my little sister do what I wanted by pinching her. Then the unspoken command came through: "Don't you dare do that again!" When I was naughty (which I'm sorry to say was quite often), she seemed to have "eagle eyes."

On the other hand, my mother's eyes sent plenty of pleasant messages, too. I remembered that when I was in a benevolent mood and did something nice, her eyes would become quite beautiful. Gently softening and glowing warmly, they would say, "I'm proud of you; keep it up." Countless times her eyes whispered across the room, "I love you."

That night, Psalm 32:8 came to mind as I thought about Mother's eyes, and I realized that God guides us with His eyes too. Although God does not actually teach us through His eyes, the consciousness of them often communicated to me things I had previously learned through His Word. It was as if He, too, was reminding me of what He expected by warning and challenging me. Admittedly, during such times I wanted to make sure there was something between God and me to intercept His messages. At other times, He has encouraged and loved me by the thought that He was watching what I was doing. 2 Chronicles 16:9 expresses the same thought: *"For the eyes of the Lord run to and fro throughout the whole earth, to show Himself strong in the behalf of them whose heart is perfect toward Him."*

Recently these thoughts reoccurred to me when I awoke in the middle of the night with an impending feeling of gloom and was absolutely consumed by fear. I suddenly felt the glow of His warm, loving eyes. It was very real to me. I could almost hear Him say, *"It is I, be not afraid!"* (Matt. 14:27). This thought gave me fresh assurance that my future and the futures of my physical and spiritual families are in His hands. Within a few minutes, I was sound asleep, resting in His love and His ability to look after every need I might have. I woke up two hours later, completely refreshed.

It's reassuring to know that, unlike the eyes of the people we love on earth, His eyes will never be dimmed by age. He will never lose His alertness. When I feel His smile of approval, it means, "Keep up the good work."

22
GOD'S INCREDIBLE PROVISION

The day we set out for China is indelibly impressed on my mind. We were one happy family. Dad had received a big smile from his first grandchild that morning, and they were having a grand time together. The thought that made it so wonderful was that my father had not only seen my birth but Ruthie's birth as well, because even before I was born he had been sent home from the hospital with the prognosis that there was no hope for him. He was happy to know we were leaving to serve the Lord, knowing that it was an answer to his and Mother's prayers of many years. They had often prayed that God would call me into His service. However, they did have mixed emotions. It was not easy for them to watch us pack the car, take their grandchild, and slowly pull out of the driveway, knowing that China in 1947 was not a safe place to take a family.

There is one more reason I shall never forget that day: our financial situation. I highly doubt that my parents would have consented to our leaving had they been aware of it. We were leaving for the West Coast on our way to China with ten dollars in our pockets. We did have the blessing of the Lord from the elders in our assembly and their promise to back us in prayer and to support us financially when possible. A few missionary meetings were scheduled with invitations to stay in the homes of Christians along the way.

I'm sure I never would have had the courage to leave home at all had I known a blizzard awaited us in Oklahoma that would cause us to stay in a motel two extra nights. In short, even with the added expense, the Lord provided for each mile of the way and He confirmed to us that He was looking out for us.

Six weeks later, Gifford, Ruthie, and I arrived in Oakland, California with ten dollars—exactly the same amount we had in hand the day we left my parents' home in Florida. We had not missed one meal, nor had we been embarrassed in any way. However, it was now much closer to our sailing date, and we still didn't have the amount of money we needed for a deposit on our tickets to China. (Please don't misunderstand me. I am not suggesting that anyone else leave for the mission field under similar circumstances. I am only sharing the way in which God provided in our unique situation.)

It would be nice if I could claim to have had constant peace during the days before our departure, but I cannot. I repeatedly struggled with the temptation to talk my husband into cancelling the reservations. However, Gifford had such peace and confidence that our timing was of the Lord that his faith kept me going. Many times afterward, I thanked God that I hadn't let my doubts hinder us or cause Gifford's strong convictions to waver. During the two short years we were able to be in China, we had the joy of working with a great team of missionaries and saw much blessing.

As we waited on the West Coast, speaking at missionary meetings, we made many interested friends. Little by little, money came in and we were able to make the deposit on the tickets, but the entire amount did not come to us until the day before our sailing date. That morning we received a cable from a friend in Florida (who was not aware of our situation) which stated that he had sold a house and was wiring his tithe to us. This sizable gift made it possible to ship our car to Shanghai, too.

A friend of ours went with Gifford to the bank and co-signed all the personal checks that had come in to meet our expenses, and we collected the wired money. Next Gifford and our friend went to the shipping office and laid fourteen one-hundred-dollar bills on the counter. The agent laughingly said, "What did you do? Rob a bank?"

Gifford, in all seriousness answered, "No, God sent it to us." You can imagine the hearty laugh with which the agent received that comment.

Eighteen days later, upon arriving in Shanghai, Gifford was ecstatic. China was the land of his birth, as he was the son of missionaries and had lived there with his family for his first fifteen years. He was home again!

Realizing very quickly how impractical a low-swung car would be on dirt roads, Gifford traded the car for a Jeep. We had enough money left over to ship the Jeep, along with all our other baggage, down the Yangtze River to our mission station. A royal welcome from our missionary family in Kweiyang, Kweichow, soon put my heart to rest and made up for the apprehension I had felt previously. The incredible way in which the Lord had multiplied our ten dollars to meet our needs for the trip across the States, our time in Oakland and Shanghai, the purchase of our tickets and opportunity to freight our personal belongings including the car, fortified me for the next two years in China and thirty-eight years in Japan.

"*...Be content with such things as ye have: for He hath said, I will never leave thee, nor forsake thee. So that we may boldly say, The Lord is my helper...*" (Heb. 13:5-6).

23
GOD'S TAPE RECORDER

We once had an interesting guest in our home, a missionary from Taiwan. He was fascinated by gadgets and, because of the nature of his missionary work, had spent a day in Akihabara, Tokyo, looking for new electrical equipment. When he returned to our home that evening, he proudly displayed the great find of the day—a clever, new tape recorder that was controlled by sound. Having no push buttons or remote control wires, it merely started to record when someone spoke. We admired it, but it wasn't until the next day that its great possibilities were demonstrated to us and we realized how wonderful a device it was.

The following morning, having completely forgotten about the recorder, we gathered around the breakfast table. We were happy that our early teenage children were home from boarding school for the weekend, and we had much to talk about. When the meal was finished, our visitor asked us, "How would you like to hear everything you've just said for the last half hour?" We looked at him in amazement and then at each other as we mentally reviewed our conversation.

The twinkle in his eye soon brought to mind the tape recorder he had shown us. He had come downstairs before any of us had awakened and had hidden the recorder behind the piano. He was able to replay everything we'd said that morning. Not even a cough or giggle was left out! Fortunately, everyone had been in a congenial, jovial mood, so it was fun to hear what we had said.

For our family that morning, there was no embarrassment

for what we had said, only pleasure. But it easily could have been very different. It wouldn't have been pleasant at all to have heard a rehearsal of bickering and fighting that stemmed from jealousies.

Now, if man is clever enough to invent a marvelous machine to record voices, is there any reason to believe that God is any less clever? Wouldn't His methods be even more effective? This is a sobering, challenging thought. Surely His computers are state-of-the-art!

Malachi tells us, *"Then they that feared the Lord spake often one to another: and the Lord hearkened, and heard it, and a book of remembrance was written before Him for them that feared the Lord, and that thought upon His name"* (Mal. 3:16). This verse is wonderfully encouraging. Every conversation that is centered on God and His precious Son, Jesus Christ, has been—and will continue to be—recorded. This verse also challenges me to remember that the Lord is not only keeping records of my words but of my thoughts as well. I can hardly imagine being rewarded for every good thought I have concerning the righteousness and goodness of God. I only regret that there are not many more to record!

Christ warned His disciples that God would, in a coming day, repeat all that had been said. I'm wondering how many things I will hear replayed that will cause me to say, "Did I actually say that?" I'm afraid I'll be surprised at the zest with which some things were said, too, for my tone is not always kind. Let's be careful to make sure that all we say will be worth repeating and will bring joy to Him and to us.

24
GRAVECLOTHES AND THE ABUNDANT LIFE

Just prior to raising Lazarus from the dead, Christ declared that He was the Good Shepherd who would give His life for His sheep. He added that He came to give life by shedding His blood for them—and not merely giving them life but *abundant* life. When visiting the home after Lazarus had died, He made an amazing statement to Martha. He said, *"I am the resurrection and the life"* (John 11:25).

Immediately after this, He called Lazarus forth from his grave. Lazarus miraculously responded, although how he wiggled himself out puzzles me. As I see Lazarus in this account, he was standing among his sisters, friends, and relatives. He was alive, but restricted in his movements by graveclothes. If I understand correctly, these were yards and yards of bandage-like cloth strips wound tightly around his body. Christ raised him, but he was still tightly bound from head to foot with his graveclothes.

I really don't think we have to look very hard or stretch our imaginations to find many people who, like Lazarus, are still all bound up in spiritual graveclothes. They have been given eternal life from the dead through their response to Christ's call, but they are not yet free from their graveclothes. I'm sure Christ would give us the same command He gave to those gathered around Lazarus: *"Loose him, and let him go."*

We who surround these people have been given a responsibility to try to free them from the old influencess that restrict them in their Christian life. They can only be freed when we do as Isaiah recommended—teach the Word of

God, precept upon precept, line upon line, here a little and there a little, so that inch by inch the graveclothes become loose enough for the person to free himself through the power of the Holy Spirit if he so wishes. Sometimes a person bound in the graveclothes of sin can become free immediately, but other times it is a slow, hard, long process.

The Pauline Epistles are full of teaching about being freed from the sins of bitterness, anger, resentment, envy, lust, and various other sins. No matter what the cause of their bondage, people need to be freed if they are going to be useful to themselves or others. We can help by exhorting, challenging, and teaching them to observe whatsoever Christ commanded. Although it is hard to imagine a live person wanting to stay bound, some people hang on to their graveclothes for dear life, lest they be exposed.

As I write this, a dear girl Gifford and I met nearly thirty years ago comes to mind. At the time we met her, she was still dead in her sins. She had suffered for years from depression, but was gloriously saved and given new life by the Lord Jesus Christ. For a period of time, her behavior improved, but it wasn't long before old problems began to surface again. There were periods during which she improved to the place of being able to hold a job for months, but eventually she would be back in depression and quit her job. Finally she got to the place of shutting herself up in her room.

One of her obvious problems was being consumed with jealousy and anger toward her whole family because of the feeling that the family had favored her younger brother above her. His bright, bubbly personality made him special in school, in the community, and among relatives. The more his popularity was accentuated, the more of a recluse she became.

One Sunday afternoon, I visited her and found her lying in bed with the shutters closed. Leaving the lights off, I could hardly see enough to find a place to sit beside her bed. We talked for hours. I explained to her that no matter how responsible others were for her situation, she was responsible for her reaction to it. I mentioned the jealousy she had toward her brother and her anger toward her parents. I tried to get her to see that her anger was really aimed at God because God had placed her in her family and had given her family members their respective personalities and abilities. Finally, feeling that there was no way to get her to let loose of her graveclothes because she was only struggling to keep them more tightly wound around her, I gave up.

In dejection I started to leave. Suddenly, the Lord put a thought into my head and I turned and asked her if she liked darkness and if she really wanted to live in darkness for the rest of her life, as she was doing at that time. She was silent for a long time, but when I stood to leave the room, her arm went up and she threw the heavily padded quilt (a Japanese futon) off her head and said simply, "No, I don't." She got up and got dressed. I left rejoicing and feeling greatly encouraged.

For a time after that, she made great progress. Although some graveclothes had been loosened, I was pretty sure something still bound her, for she did not move around among the Christians as a free person, much less as a person who possessed abundant life.

Some time later, she came to me one night, desperately in tears. She told me of a sin in her past from which she could not feel forgiven nor free herself. Again that night, the Lord put a suggestion in my mind.

Taking her to an empty room and asking her to sit down at a desk, I asked her to write out all the details of her sin on paper. I told her not to spare any of the feelings of enjoyment that had in any way contributed to the sin. Then I left her to work. A half hour later, she was still not finished. An hour later, I heard sobbing. Finally, I could hear the sobbing subside. Then I walked in, and I knew the battle had been won.

One look at her smile through her tears showed that she had decided to throw off a few more of the graveclothes.

Seeing this fruit of repentance, I asked her to please give me the papers. Without even glancing at them, I tore them in half, in quarters, and into tiny pieces. The two of us walked to a small irrigation ditch that lined my property. I handed the pieces to her and asked her to drop them into the rushing water. She did. We stood for a second in the moonlight, then I told her to pick up the pieces again. She looked at me, nonplussed, and said, "That's impossible." Her demeanor brightened as she got the point. In the same way that those little pieces of paper had irretrievably disappeared, her sins were gone beyond reach.

After walking back to the house, we opened our Bibles to Micah 7:19. Before we read this portion, I asked her where she thought those pieces of paper were by that time. She thought they had probably floated out to the creek. Then I asked her where they would be the next day. Her reply was, "In the river." My next question was "Where from there?" After a long, thoughtful pause she replied, "They would go to the ocean." We then read, "Thou wilt cast all their sins into the depths of the sea." It was the thrill of a lifetime to watch her face as the truth of those words sunk in. All her sins were in the depths of the sea—just like those pieces of paper soon would be.

She enrolled in a school for further training, got a good job, and stuck it out until she worked herself into a responsible position. Now, more then ten years later, she is a wife, a mother, and a productive Christian. Since Christ paid such a high price to give her eternal life, it would have been a pity for her to have spent the rest of her life bound in graveclothes instead of being able to enjoy the abundant life He offers.

25
GREAT FAITH

An ordinary woman from the crowd approached Jesus one day to ask for the healing of her daughter. In fact, in the eyes of the Jews surrounding Christ, she wasn't even an ordinary woman; she was a despised Gentile. Yet, Christ not only granted her request, He complimented her for her faith and added that it was "great" faith (Matt. 15:21-28).

This comment aroused my curiosity. What was so great about this Canaanite woman's faith? I wondered. As I reread the passage, I didn't notice any personal, outstanding characteristics, nor did Matthew mention that she had any special abilities or achievements. What then did Christ see in her faith that so pleased Him? How did her faith differ from that of other women who crowded around Him? She was persistent, but dozens of other persistent women got what they asked of Him without receiving praise for their faith.

Wanting to discover how I could stretch my faith to the point of winning the Lord's approval, I read the story again. When I did, I saw the woman's faith stretched before my very eyes as the story unfolded. Her reactions to what the Lord said and did drew His attention. First, the Lord was silent and seemed to ignore her completely, but she didn't let this bother her nor did she give up. Second, she knew well what He meant when He referred to those not of the "lost sheep of the house of Israel," but she responded, not by hurt feelings, but by worshipping Him. Instead of letting His statement deter her, she agreed with Him and continued her plea even more earnestly, reminding Him that even the dogs get their share of the food that falls from their Master's table. His silence and seemingly unsympathetic attitude seemed to encourage her faith rather than cause her to turn away.

Right from the beginning, she called Jesus "Lord" and referred to Him as the "Son of David." By this she acknowledged Him as the Messiah. She was confident that, as God, He could do anything for her and that He, as sovereign, had the prerogative to choose when, how, and whom He would heal. Acknowledging Him as Lord and at the same time admitting she deserved nothing from Him because she was not of the right nationality caused Christ to praise her. She was willing (figuratively) to take her place under the table with the dogs to eat with thankfulness and satisfaction the crumbs that fell from the Master's hands. She did not question why she had seemingly been discriminated against. Rather, she accepted her position and on the basis of it asked for mercy.

An invalid friend of mine is one of the greatest women of faith I know. I have known her for more than thirty years. After receiving a tract one day while in the hospital, she read it and was touched by the thought that while on the cross Christ prayed that the Father would forgive His murderers. She contrasted her bitter, angry self with His forgiving response to suffering.

If ever a woman had a right to bear resentment, she did. She, her husband, and four children lived in Manchuria during the China-Japanese war. They returned to Japan at the end of the war with their one surviving son. Soon after their return, she was hospitalized with tuberculosis of the spine. When her husband heard her prognosis, he divorced her without explanation. He refused to take any responsibility for her, married her dearest and closest friend, and moved to South America, taking her only son. Her immediate family, fearing they would have to care for her financially, refused to have any contact with her. She was left sick, destitute, and heartbroken.

Yet, as she read of Christ's forgiving heart in the face of great injustice, she became convicted of her resentment. Confessing this sin, she became truly saved. Her faith grew by leaps and bounds, although at the time she was too weak to even hold a Bible in her hands. During the thirty years of our friendship I have visited her countless times. Never once, that I can remember, have I heard her complain of her lot in life. Often being spiritually dry, discouraged, or disgruntled myself, I never returned home without having caught some of her infectious joy in knowing Christ personally. To this day, she has a consistent, vital relationship with Him that challenges me, is a tremendous testimony to other patients, and is an example to the Christian young people who visit her. She has never lost the wonder of the peace she received at her salvation. She has an unwavering belief that the sufferings of this life are not worthy to be compared with the glory of eternity (see Rom. 8:18).

Both my dear friend and the Syrophoenician woman are wonderful examples of people who clearly express their faith by their complete dependence on the Lord. They trust His goodness and His wise judgment, although it may seem contrary to human thinking. They honestly admit before God their inability and unworthiness, recognizing Him for who He really is. They both agreed that they were impotent and He was omnipotent. May we join these two dear women in our praise and worship under all circumstances, knowing that we will also be commended as having great faith if we do this.

26
HELPING GOD OUT

It is with mixed emotions that I think of Rebekah. On one hand, when I read about her in Genesis 24, I admire her, seeing her as an energetic, kind girl who was always ready to help a stranger. On the other hand, when reading further, there are some disappointments. But first let's consider her positive qualities.

When a stranger approached Rebekah one day at the well and asked for water, she noticed that his camels needed a drink, too, and volunteered to draw water for them—no small task. The stranger then proceeded to talk about God and made a proposal for her to marry his master's son. After receiving the approval of her family, she trusted God enough to set off on a journey to a land she had never seen, with a man she didn't know, to marry someone she had never met. This took real courage and shows us that she was an outstanding young woman who had strong determination and faith. Plus the fact that after the marriage she soon won Isaac's heart (v. 67) and comforted him after the death of his mother, speaks well for her ability to be a good wife.

Yet, after we finish reading about these wonderful qualities, we see Rebekah in Genesis 27, now in middle age, deceiving Isaac. We feel let down. In one chapter, she steps out and demonstrates strong faith; in the other, she limits God, which gives evidence of a lack of faith.

I don't sanction her deceit, no matter what her motives were, but I sympathize with her because I am inclined to think that a feeling of panic pushed her into her deception. I think she felt she had to ensure that Jacob, not Esau, received the family inheritance with his father's blessing. I would even go so far as to say she thought she was "helping" God to fulfill His promise concerning the two boys.

Before the boys were born, we remember that God had told her Esau would serve Jacob and lose his right as the firstborn son. As she and Isaac approached their latter years, Rebekah saw that the promise was still unfulfilled and felt she was the only one who could rectify the situation. Time was growing short because Isaac was old and growing older. Rebekah really panicked when she overheard a conversation between Isaac and Esau that would make it impossible for Jacob, the right son, to receive the blessing.

In her way of thinking, the deadline had come. Esau, not Jacob, would get the blessing that God had promised. Rebekah was sure that once the blessing was pronounced, God's plan would be thwarted. Esau had already proven himself unworthy to assume the spiritual responsibility that accompanied the blessing because he had sold his birthright and had married a pagan woman. As far as Rebekah was concerned, things had gotten out of control, so she took the situation into her own hands. She deceived Isaac into thinking that Jacob was Esau.

I identify with Rebekah's frustration because I have often been in similar situations and felt that God was working far too slowly. I have even thought that He would be disgraced and lose face if I didn't come to His rescue or at least give Him a little help (though I would not have said that out loud).

Rebekah paid dearly for her scheming and for not waiting for God to work on Jacob's behalf. (Admittedly, it did look pretty hopeless.) She lost Jacob completely when he had to flee the country in order to save his life. After her favorite son—her pride and joy—had to leave home, she must have endured many long, sad hours. The consequences of limiting

God's ability were costly. Rebekah died before Jacob was able to safely return home.

Ironically, Isaac was alive and well when Jacob returned many years later. I wonder how many blessings I have cheated myself out of by scheming instead of believing God to work in His time and way. I find great comfort in the thought however, and I rest assured that even though Rebekah limited God, He was fully able to overrule her mistakes. True, Jacob was lost to her, but he was not lost to the Lord. Though Rebekah did not live to enjoy or share in any of Jacob's blessings, God, in His sovereign grace, continued to work in Jacob's life for blessing until all of His promises regarding Jacob were fulfilled. God finished what He had begun.

27
HIS SERVANTS WILL SERVE HIM

The thoughts expressed in Revelation 22:3 have at times been a tremendous comfort to me: *"There shall be no more curse: but the throne of God and of the Lamb shall be in it; and His servants shall serve Him."*

I first noticed this verse in a special way soon after my husband went to be with the Lord. There are few things that make one think about heaven—and in what form the saints exist while they are waiting for their resurrected bodies—more than having a loved one go there. For days after my husband died, I could think of nothing else.

I knew Gifford was with Christ and that was a wonderful consolation, but I had a hard time imagining just what he was doing. He had always been occupied with projects for the Lord (the bigger the better). To be busy had been one of his greatest joys, so I wondered how he would occupy his time. Then I picked up the Bible and happened to read, *"His servants shall serve Him."* This sentence captivated me. As I sat back to meditate on it, I soon was caught up in the thrill of knowing it didn't really matter what form he had. He was, after all, serving God. Knowing Gifford, he was happy, and I could imagine his smiling face as he praised and worshipped God. For him, to live on earth had been Christ, and I knew this was still true. Christ, not the work for Christ, mattered most. What joy for Gifford, and what comfort for me. Worship and praise, after all, are the ultimate service.

The second time the Lord brought this verse to mind was at my mother's bedside. She was extremely ill with two blood clots and was suffering greatly. My sister and I stood beside her that evening, and I cried out to the Lord with all my heart that He would take her to be with Himself. For a few minutes, I harbored a feeling of resentment because He didn't immediately take her out of her misery. The thought passed through my mind: Lord, she is just too good a women to suffer like this.

It may seem strange, but at that very moment Revelation 22:3 flashed before me. In an instant, with that thought, I received a tiny glimpse as to why the Lord might be leaving her here a little longer. This life is only a training ground for eternity. Since her character was the only thing she would take with her, the Lord was causing a bit more iron to enter her soul as training for eternal service. I highly doubted that He would be training her for future service in this world at the age of ninety-two. I also realized that the training period might possibly be for us—her children—and not for her at all.

It seemed to me that learning acceptance, submission, and patience was a top priority with God in His training program for His saints. He was using this experience of enduring pain to prepare her (and my sister and me) just a bit better for eternal service. Special service requires special training and fortitude. I believe that He is more interested in building our character than in providing comfort here on earth. Even Mother was not exempt.

As I discussed this thought with a friend a few days later, the question arose as to why special training is necessary, since the moment we enter eternity we lose our sinful, rebellious natures. We wondered why God would spend so much effort and time in training us for something He will do in an instant. After mulling over this question for weeks, I became more convinced than ever that the Lord builds our character in this life with eternity in view. He has special purposes for doing so before He removes the curse of sin.

When we serve Him in heaven, our placement will not be

based on our abilities, gifts, or talents but rather on our character. I have concluded that our position in heaven will be determined by how much we allow God to develop our character and by the submission we have learned here on earth. Obeying, taking responsibility, being faithful, and loving will be the criteria for service there.

To someone like Gifford, being naturally energetic and highly motivated, service was no strain. To another, like my mother, who was seemingly born with a submissive, obedient temperament, yielding to the perfect will of God seems to be no problem. However, to those of us who were not endowed with either abundant energy or a submissive temperament, eternal service could become drudgery if we were still under sin's curse. But the blessed words, "There shall be no more curse," is enough to quicken the pulse as I pictured myself serving Him. All laziness, weaknesses of the flesh, and all stubbornness and rebellion will be erased in a moment when God removes the curse of sin.

It gives great joy to think that not only will the curse be taken from me but I will be working only with others who have been freed from the curse as well. There will be no personality conflicts and no more dragging of the feet. Nothing will hinder the sheer pleasure and great delight of serving Him forever.

28
HOPE DELAYED

I had an unusual experience recently. Within a couple of days, the same verse of Scripture was quoted to me twice under similar circumstances. The way it was quoted impressed me, because in both cases one friend in a group started to quote the verse, *"Hope deferred maketh the heart sick..."* and a second person piped up to finish the verse, *"but when the desire cometh, it is a tree of life"* (Prov. 13:12). I thought it was strange that two people quoted the same verse within such a short period of time and that they both placed special emphasis on the second half of the verse. In addition, the verse came up in casual conversation, which gave me the impression that the Lord was emphasizing some point to me.

Since we are all well-acquainted with hopes that are delayed and the sickness of heart they cause, I was pretty sure that the Lord wasn't bringing dashed hopes to my attention. Rather, what I did while I was waiting for my hope to come was what was important to Him. The necessity of letting Him produce a tree of life and learning what I could about Him while waiting for it to arrive interested Him. Trees are supposed to produce fruit and provide shade, and both of these benefits are meant to be shared.

I considered two vivid Old Testament examples of fruit being produced through long delays. Both Sarah and Hannah waited a long time to have their hopes and desires fulfilled. Sarah waited twenty-five years for her "hoped for" baby, Isaac, and as she waited, her faith was stretched. When the baby came, it did become a tree of life, and we still see the fruit that resulted to this day. Hannah didn't have to wait for little Samuel that long, but, because she had a rival in the home who made things unbearable for her, her agony was intense. The fruit we enjoy from these two trees is sweet. As we read their stories, we are encouraged never to lose hope. It is never too late for God to work.

Both of these women were rejuvenated to the extent that when their desires were fulfilled, they became very productive. Sarah was so invigorated by her faith, which had been stretched through many years of waiting, that she was able to see the baby grow into adulthood, even though she was ninety years old when he was born. I especially like the verse in Hebrews, which says that Sarah's faith (not Abraham's) gave her the strength for birth.

As in Sarah's case, faith often gives physical strength as well as emotional strength. Hannah, for example, started a whole family through the energy she received after the birth of her "hoped for" Samuel. Her prayer of praise enlightens us with some of the things she learned about God while waiting for her desire to be fulfilled. Some of these are: He is alive, He is holy, and He is a rock of strength; the Lord is sovereign, and He gives strength to and preserves His children.

Perhaps I should mention Mary and Martha, too. Although their hope was only delayed a short time, it was so intense that for a period of time they even gave up hope after their brother, Lazarus, died. They had hoped desperately that Christ would arrive in time to heal Lazarus, but He didn't. Reading between the lines, they accused the Lord of not coming to be with them when they needed Him the most. These words, *"If thou hadst been here, my brother had not died"* (John 11:21), are rather surprising coming from the lips of Martha, who had such a close friendship with the Lord. They express the anguish of heart she experienced when her hopes were shattered. It is even more surprising to hear Mary—the loving, quiet, trusting one—say exactly the same thing a few minutes later (John 11:32). When Mary and Martha had given up hope, their emotions were stretched to the breaking point. They as much as said, "Lord, You are just too late. There is nothing you can do now. He's dead." Many of us at some point have also felt that Christ has let us down.

All four of these women gave into their feelings of desperation and frustration at some time but came out victorious because they had an underlying faith in God. Sarah certainly had her failures. Hannah, too, gave in to intense self-pity, and Mary and Martha became very upset with the Lord. They all had times of weakness. But when God encouraged them, through His Word, they hung onto their hope and all of them were rewarded. For Mary and Martha, the scenario completely changed within minutes. Their hopes were revived, and the Lord responded to their need by raising Lazarus from the dead. For Sarah, the fulfillment took twenty-five years. It is God who sets time limits.

During the two or three days I've been thinking about the necessity of having to wait on Christ until a desired hope arrives, some very special tulips have been opening up for me. I've been waiting impatiently for them to blossom and realize that had I tried to open the buds prematurely with my clumsy fingers, I would only have torn them to shreds. Slowly I've seen what sunshine and refreshing rain have done to these blossoms. They are now beautiful. I recall that God also has worked out certain family circumstances and church situations that looked pretty hopeless and developed them into something that was beautiful and promising.

Many times, when I think God is taking too much time to bring my hopes to fruition, I encourage myself by thinking of the Book of Esther in which God works behind the scenes all the time. Someone has said that when God works silently, He is moving to change the scenes.

We'd do well to let God have the freedom to work in the same way, at His pace, without our intervention. By direct contrast, if God were to give us all of the things we hope for and fulfill our desires when and how we want them, there is the possibility that it would produce leanness of soul instead of a tree of life. *"He gave them their request; but sent leanness into their soul"* (Ps. 106:15). The matter of having our hopes delayed is not our choice, but we can choose whether our fulfilled hopes turn into a tree that spreads forth branches for fruit and shade or whether our hopes cause leanness to enter our own souls and shrivel our spiritual life. It is our desire that we may produce fruit for refreshment and to be a shady spot for those feeling the heat and toil of the day.

29
JOSEPH SPOKE KINDLY

Today I read Exodus 39:14, *"And the stones were according to the names of the children of Israel, twelve, according to their names."* These stones shone from the breastplate of the high priest as he ministered before the Lord in the tabernacle, to remind Him of His chosen people—the twelve tribes that descended from the sons of Jacob. As I read, I wondered if the names would have sparkled before the Lord like this so many generations later if the brothers of Joseph had not made things right with him (see Gen. 37-50.) I highly doubt they would have. Jacob would not have had the opportunity to bless his sons if they had not confessed their guilt. The whole of history was changed because the brothers admitted their wrong and Joseph forgave them.

Genesis 50:21 states simply, *"He comforted them, and spake kindly unto them."* Under normal circumstances, we wouldn't be surprised by the fact that he spoke kindly, because he was talking to his brothers. But these were not normal circumstances.

Joseph had more than twenty years to brood, if he had chosen to do so, over what his brothers had done to him. His brothers had rejected him because of their jealousy over his dreams and their father's partiality. He had years to dwell on the kidnapping, their plan of murder, and their selling him as a slave. In spite of this, although he was an innocent victim, he didn't brood.

If ever a person would have been justified in saying, "I can't forgive them," Joseph was that person. Yet we find him speaking kindly to his brothers. Joseph did not react to their cruel actions, although he was certainly in a position to do so. He hadn't wasted any time cultivating grudges for past wrongs done against him, even though his brother's injustice had been to the nth degree.

Instead, Joseph kept himself well occupied with business at hand, thus finding his acceptance and identification through fellowship with God. He knew that God was with him and was blessing him. In whatever circumstances he found himself, he was soon placed in the position of manager—even in prison. When Joseph's brothers admitted their guilt, he was ready to forgive them. Not only did he speak to them kindly, but he also treated them royally by making provision for their future. That is what I call a perfect example of going the second mile—and then some.

It has been said that there are as many sins of reaction as of initial action. Sometimes the reactions are even more hurtful and sinful than the original wrong that was committed. Many people have become bitter for far less significant reasons, but Joseph didn't. Instead, he learned to sympathize with his brothers by permitting God to become real to him during the years he suffered from the memories of their cruelty and indifference to his pleas for mercy. Through experiencing God's work in his heart, he realized that they were imprisoned, too. He knew theirs was not a prison of brick and mortar but one of a guilty conscience, which is equally as bad or worse. He felt sorry for them. He fought to keep back his tears all the time they were asking him for grain and did not know who he was. He longed for fellowship with them.

When Joseph saw his brothers arrive in Egypt, no doubt he wanted to ask immediately about his aged father. But knowing that relationships could not return to normal until the evil done against him was rectified, he waited until they confessed their sin. Joseph knew they needed to face their father and admit that he had not been slain by wild animals after all.

He was well aware of how difficult it would be for them to confess this evil deed to their father, yet he knew the truth had to come out before there could be blessing and relief for their consciences. Joseph loved them and had their best at heart.

No doubt Joseph prayed for his brothers the whole time they returned to Canaan to get Jacob. They had the difficult task of explaining to their father what they had done to Joseph. What relief Joseph must have felt when he saw the wagons returning, carrying his father. Only then did he know his brothers had completed their mission. It was proof that they had matured to the place of taking responsibility for their wrong. He could happily continue with his plans to get them settled in and comfortably provided for in Egypt.

I think the scene of the reunion between Jacob and Joseph is one of the most touching scenes in the Bible. I love it, for I feel with them both. I have been on both sides in similar situations and can imagine the many struggles that had taken place in each heart in order to bring about this reconciliation. How delighted Jacob must have been to have his family united again.

Sibling quarrels are as old as mankind, but God's remedy for them dates back even farther. God promised to send the Redeemer through whom true unity comes. Brothers and sisters have been fighting and devouring each other since Adam's son, Cain, started the battle. Many a family feud goes on for years. This is a great pity when it can be settled so quickly through an apology, acceptance, and forgiveness.

As new missionaries, Gifford and I had an unforgettably wonderful example of unity on a mission station that was preserved through the righting of wrongs and the whole-hearted willingness to extend forgiveness. The tears flowed freely. First there were tears of heartache, then tears of joy. From that point on, we saw increased blessing on the entire mission station.

We will see, when we get to heaven, that *"the sufferings of this present time are not worthy to be compared with the glory which shall be revealed in us"* (Rom. 8:18). It is what God is able to do in the hearts of people involved on both sides of an issue that brings glory to Him. God is happy to heal breaches, but such healing requires action on both sides. Guilty people must be willing to admit their sin and apologize; those who are wronged must be just as willing to accept the apology. If they do, all the names of those involved will sparkle before the Lord—now and in eternity.

30
Lydia's Hospitality

As far as the Scriptures are concerned, Lydia's history began in a prayer meeting (Acts 16:12-15). The Bible reveals few personal details about Lydia, other than the fact she was a businesswoman who sold purple cloth and that she met regularly with others at the riverbank for prayer. At one of these gatherings, Paul—a visiting preacher—fully explained that the only way to God was through His blessed Son, Jesus Christ. Lydia's prepared heart readily accepted the wonderful message of salvation.

Lydia was no sooner saved and baptized than she began to serve the Lord. Immediately having the desire to entertain the Lord's servants, she did not consider hospitality to be drudgery but a highly honored privilege. Her invitation to her first guests—Paul, Silas, and Timothy—was not a casual invitation for the sake of politeness. She *begged* them to stay with her. She was concerned that she was too unworthy to have these representatives of God under her roof.

Her hospitality, as it turned out, could be counted on at any time. Once, when Paul and his companions were released from prison, they went straight to Lydia's house. No doubt this was an unexpected visit, yet they did not worry about her being inconvenienced. They had benefited from her generous hospitality in the past, so they did not worry whether their bruised and battered bodies would be an embarrassment to this refined woman. Her tender kindness and true understanding gave them the assurance that they would find a warm welcome at any time, under any circumstances. This in itself was a tribute to her graciousness and diligence. Actually, it is a compliment to any woman when her willingness to serve can safely be taken for granted.

We can all learn from Lydia's example of willing service. Peter mentions (1 Peter 4:9) that we are all to show hospitality without grudging. No doubt this includes "surprise or unplanned entertaining." I have discovered from experience that one can entertain happily ninety-nine times, but if the hostess shows agitation one time when under stress, that one time will be remembered most.

Christ mentions (Luke 14:12-14) that we are to be hospitable not only to our friends but to strangers and the less fortunate. We are to welcome the handicapped, which includes those spiritually as well as those emotionally disabled. Often the less desirable people need Christian hospitality the most.

Looking through the Scriptures, we find that hospitality usually has a purpose. For instance, it is a means to introduce someone to Christ (John 12:9), to teach individuals (Acts 18:26), to minister to the needs of others, such as ministering brethren (2 Kings 4:8-11), and for the encouragement and comfort of believers (Acts 28:30-31; 3 John 5-6). I'm sure mutual entertaining for the pure joy and relaxation in fellowship with friends is included as well.

The art of gracious entertaining is without doubt a special gift from God, but the ability to entertain is certainly not limited to those who are so gifted. It is an art that can be cultivated and is not limited to married women. Single women are often gracious hostesses. Entertaining is also not to be limited by the size or social standard of our homes. It is to be limited only by our desire to please God, for when we welcome people into our homes, Christ counts it as welcoming Him. In whatever manner we would welcome Christ, we should welcome others.

31
MODELS OF SERVANTHOOD

God was so pleased with our sister, Phoebe, that He mentioned her in Scripture by name as a "servant of the church" (Rom. 16:1-2). He didn't give details as to what she did to earn this title or what service she rendered that brought Him such joy. I would guess it was any number of duties, such as showing hospitality, visiting, teaching, helping the poor, or cleaning the kitchen. We're also not told how much time she spent in serving the church. Scripture only tells us that she was a servant.

When we think about it, we are all to be servants. It is a supreme joy to serve the Church of Jesus Christ. To be the servant of the object of Christ's love, for which He gave Himself, is an honor to be coveted by us all.

A servant can be anyone, ranging from a lowly bondslave in a private home to the highest steward in a royal household. An ambassador is even a servant, for an ambassador serves his or her country. However, no servant's position can possibly equal the honor of being a servant of the Church, the center of Christ's love.

As I think about the role of service in the body of Christ, I remember our early missionary years in China. Gifford and I lived in the hills, where servants were necessary in order to run a household smoothly. We had no running water. It had to be carried from a river a great distance away and had to be boiled and cooled before drinking. We had no electricity, so we had no electrical conveniences. Our kitchen stove was made out of mud bricks and located in a building separate from the house. It was a time-consuming chore just to keep the charcoal burning. Our goats had to be taken to the hills every day for pasture and brought home again to be milked so our babies could have milk. The market was in a different location every day. We had to bargain for every morsel of food, which took hours, and washing our clothes, diapers, and linen by hand was a full-time job. To do all of these duties, the Lord graciously provided us with three very good servants. (We paid each one the equivalent of three U.S. dollars a month.)

Truthfully, our servants' duties were not always performed to my complete satisfaction, but they certainly tried to please and asked often what we wanted done. Even today, the memory of those devoted servants warms my heart. They worked faithfully for our good.

One incident that I remember best was the night our two-year-old, Ruth, awoke writhing in pain, and the whole household responded. Even though we had not asked for their help, they stirred the fire, boiled water, and stood waiting to help in any way they could. Later, when Ruth was taken into town for surgery, the servants went on a voluntary fast until they received word that the crisis had passed.

The servants did not think of themselves, but shared in our sorrow and anxiety. They did far more than we required of them. Theirs was a service of love that I appreciate to this day. In contrast to these faithful, self-sacrificing workers who consulted with us before they did anything, we later had an independent helper who was used to doing things her way and did not bother to ask how or when we wanted it done.

For example, when a business couple returned to the States, they gave us their carpet for our living room. It had a couple of soiled places on it, but we were so grateful for the rug that we overlooked them, always hoping to shampoo it but never getting it done. Late one afternoon, we returned home to find our expensive carpet outside the house, draped over chairs and boxes of all different sizes and shapes. Without consulting us, our servant had soaked it, scrubbed it and set it out to dry. It was clean, but. . . it had dried in the hot sun to the uneven shape of the boxes and chairs! Even though she had been convinced that she was doing right, we couldn't use the rug after that.

Through this experience, I realized the importance of being in constant communication with our Master. Even though our motives are right, He may have reasons for having us wait before we do certain jobs for Him.

It is my hope that, in eternity, Christ will be able to think back to my service for Him with as warm a glow as I have when I think of our dear Chinese servants who were always so careful to receive instructions before doing new jobs. I'm sure the widow who served us didn't enjoy carting a load of dirty diapers to the river a mile away, especially when she had to break the ice to wash them. But she loved our babies and did that task without complaint. Neither did the cook appreciate getting up to stir the charcoal fire to make a pot of tea in order to serve an unexpected guest who came for help late at night. But he also did it joyfully for our sake.

I pray that my hospitality—visiting the sick and helping the poor—will be done as ungrudgingly for His sake as theirs was for us and that He will have few occasions to remember me as a servant who did not wait for His directions. I want my name on His roster of servants, and I hope He'll be able to add the two little words, "good" and "faithful" before the caption, "a servant of the Church."

32
MOTHERS OF THE FAITH

The Book of Proverbs expresses that the children of good women will rise up to call them blessed. This is as it should be and is pleasing to the Lord. In most countries, May is the month in which mothers are especially honored. Expressions of love flow freely: dinners are held, cards are sent, gifts are given, and letters are written from almost every nation in the world. So much has been written on motherhood that I don't need to add anything more. However, I would like to pay tribute to the many spiritual mothers the Lord has given to His family. Spiritual mothers who have advised, rebuked, taught, and encouraged God's children deserve honor, too.

The first example of a present-day spiritual mother who comes to my mind fits this description well. I left home as a young bride and was living in a city in which my husband and I knew absolutely no one until this dear, motherly sister invited us home to share dinner with her one Lord's day.

She took us under her wing as if we were her own family, becoming a second mother to us. This dear woman in her late seventies lived on a small pension. She was not only a spiritual help, but also in daily life. She carefully taught me much about setting up and running a home. She was genuinely interested in meeting our emotional and physical needs. She really loved us. At the time, I did not always appreciate everything she said because I had trouble admitting I needed a mentor. But when I look back, I can see that it was helpful.

The second woman who comes to mind was also elderly. She was a veteran missionary who the Lord used to encourage me by giving me much-welcomed support and good hints on managing my young family. She also gave me many hints on providing proper nourishment on a native diet. She rode the train for several hours every Friday in order to pray with me, and she always had a special tidbit from the Lord. She helped me in my early missionary service as I sorted out priorities, and guided me toward keeping a proper balance between my family and missionary service. She was also a grandmother image for our three growing daughters.

Deborah must have been this type of woman; she is referred to as a "mother" in Israel (Jud. 5:7). She had great faith and a personal interest in people. Having a close relationship with the Lord, she was able to advise others, teaching them to praise the Lord and give God the glory in victory. By working hard behind the scenes, she could stir people into action.

Spiritual motherhood has no limitations of age or marital status. Two verses verify that. Psalms 92:14 says, *"They shall still bring forth fruit in old age."* Isaiah 54:1 states, *"More are the children of the desolate than the children of the married wife."* Many decisions for salvation have been made over a cup of coffee shared by a devoted, caring sister and a person who has a seeking heart. Many a discouraged person has been lifted up through the counsel of a sensitive woman. Temptations have been avoided as the result of personal interest; struggling babes in Christ have been strengthened. An example might be a timid individual who is encouraged to attend a Bible study or gospel service. In some cases, being a spiritual mother might even mean making it possible for a person to attend such events. There is also no limit to the spiritual growth stimulated through profitable reading materials that have been given according to the Holy Spirit's prompting. Following the example of physical mothers who patiently make themselves available at all times and expect nothing in return, I am challenged by these good spiritual mothers. I, for one, rise up to call them blessed.

33
OBEDIENT BUT REBELLIOUS ZIPPORAH

Moses and his wife, Zipporah, had just had an encounter with God in which He had rebuked them for neglecting the sacred rite of circumcision. Zipporah immediately obeyed by circumcising their son, but after doing so, s*he turned on her husband in anger with the stinging words, "Surely a bloody husband art thou to me"* (Ex. 4:25). I can just see the hurt look on Moses' face as he wilted under her unfair accusation. Zipporah had no mercy when she accused Moses of being a bloody man.

I think many women today would naturally agree that circumcision seems to be a cruel act, but since circumcision was not Moses' idea, Zipporah did not need to take the anger out on him. Her anger was really directed at God. Many of God's laws were hard to understand and would seem difficult to us today, but God only reminded them of a law they had failed to honor.

God had given explicit instructions regarding circumcision way back in Abraham's time. The Israelites had been in Egypt for many years, but now He was bringing them into the Promised Land. Circumcision was a seal of His covenant with them, so He reminded them of the importance of keeping this law before they could enter the land. God wanted Moses to reinstate this rite, beginning with his own family.

God had previously said that anyone refusing circumcision was to be cut off from his people, and Moses was no exception. Therefore God met Moses and sought to take his life because of his neglect in this area. Just what God did to

Moses we don't know. Whatever it was, He must have inca-pacitated Moses to the extent that he couldn't circumcise the child himself, so Zipporah did it. Zipporah obeyed, but the spirit with which she did so was rebellious and angry.

Scripture does not specifically tell us, but perhaps due to her attitude she was sent back to her father's home soon after this incident, thus forfeiting her opportunity to be the help-mate God intended her to be. God had asked Moses to take on the colossal job of leading His people out of Egypt and back to Canaan. Moses very much needed the support of a faithful, loving wife because he felt insecure and unqualified for the position. Zipporah's anger and rebellion, however, made that impossible.

I view Zipporah as a negative example of that which we should avoid today. Many of our husbands are leaders in the churches of God and have been given implicit instructions for building it, thus they sorely need our loving support. Some-times we wives don't understand perfectly all the "whys" of God's requirements. We also find that what God expects from us is often hard to take, especially when it cuts across the grain of human reasoning and invites criticism and misun-derstanding. We would do well to remember that we have a responsibility to stand behind not only our spouses, but all of our leaders who are consciously trying to follow God's will and carry out His instructions. Whether we understand what is expected of them or not, we should give them continued prayer support. We need to remember, as James informs us, *"The wrath of man worketh not the righteousness of God"* (James 1:20). We need to strive to obey God with the right attitude. More than once I've prayed, "Lord, even though I'm still kicking and screaming inside, please don't give up on me. Bring my rebellious heart into subjection." We don't want to follow Zipporah's poor example of being obedient—but still rebellious and angry.

34
RAHAB: A LESSON ON WAITING

At times God uses the most unlikely individuals to fulfill His purposes. The harlot, Rahab, for instance, is known as a woman who made her living through sinful practices. Yet God used her to house and protect His servants when they were on a special mission for Him (see Josh. 2). Through her clever scheme, she saved the lives of God's servants by hiding them on her roof. Because of her kindness, her name has been preserved; it is even included in Matthew's genealogy of our wonderful Saviour and Lord, Jesus Christ.

Although Rahab's profession was nothing to be proud of, she must have been a very intelligent and truth-seeking woman. When the news spread through Jericho that the Israelites were coming, she listened with all her heart and accepted the news of their previous victories with the simplest faith possible. When God's men appeared, she asked no questions but merely said, *"For the Lord your God, He is God in heaven above, and in earth beneath"* (Josh. 2:11). From that simple but firm foundation, her faith grew.

Rahab's faith soon grew to envelop her family. Not satisfied to be spared alone, she immediately asked for the protection of her whole family. This spoke eloquently of the type of person she was. She had great concern for her family. Each family member had to make an individual choice to stay in the house behind the scarlet cord in order to be saved from destruction, yet Rahab convinced them all to stay with her.

Rahab's story is one of the most beautiful pictures of faith put into practice. The fact she is later mentioned three times in the New Testament indicates that her faith continued to mature as she determined to make the living God of Israel her God. She not only changed her lifestyle but her identity, and she did so by leaving the doomed city of Jericho to join forces with the people of God. She truly was a treasure hidden in a despised, earthen vessel.

This woman of amazing faith may have had anxious moments while waiting for the fulfillment of the promise of protection given by the men of God. It certainly could not have been easy to remain in the house and live on a wall that she was sure would tumble down. She had not been given details of how God planned to preserve her small section of the wall. As the Israelite army walked around the city in silence, she surely thought that was a mighty strange strategy. She may have even been annoyed at times with the awful, unbearable silence, and wondered why the battle was delayed day after day while the Israelites marched around the city.

Had I been Rahab, I'm sure I would have been out many times examining the wall for cracks, checking to measure God's progress in crumbling the wall. We don't know whether Rahab waited with perfect peace and trust or whether she waited in fretful frustration. However, we know that her attitude didn't affect her safety. God had made a promise to her, and He fulfilled it. Her feelings and fears had nothing to do with her safety. Her obedience in staying behind the scarlet cord was all that mattered. She stayed there to the very end when the Israelites came to bring her and her family out of the house (Josh. 6:22-23).

Likewise, Christ has promised to return to take you and me out of this condemned world. We are under orders to watch and pray until that day. Whether we do so in peaceful trust or in fretful frustration, our attitude will not affect our safety. The choice is ours as to how we will occupy our time while we wait for the end to approach. The prophecies found in Daniel and Matthew can be frightening, but instead of being consumed by worry and anxiety about how the house will come down when the wall crumbles, we can be occupied with persuading our families, friends, and neighbors to come in with us behind the scarlet cord—a symbol of Christ's redemptive blood. Certain members of our family will find it harder than others to stay under His protection, so we should encourage them to be patient until He comes.

There are two main reasons why some people find the confinement harder than others: boredom and fear of what might come. It is our responsibility to encourage those who are tempted to scout around in the doomed city to stay under shelter. We also have the responsibility to encourage the fearful ones. Christ told us not to be troubled but rather to look up, knowing that our redemption gets nearer every day. We are to encourage others that the God who is wise and powerful enough to bring prophecy to fulfillment is capable of protecting us while the walls come tumbling down. In doing so, our own faith will be greatly stengthened.

35
RUFOUS, A BROWN HUMMINGBIRD

While we were visiting the United States on furlough, a friend offered us the use of her cabin in the mountains for a week. She wanted my daughters and me to have the opportunity to enjoy each other again after years of separation. The cabin, nestled in a beautiful Rocky Mountain canyon, was surrounded on three sides by ever-changing color as the shadows were transformed on the rugged rocks hour by hour. My friend's ranch was stocked with cattle, and there was plenty of wildlife to enjoy. We watched chipmunks, deer, coyotes, and other creatures. It was fun to follow their antics.

When we weren't hiking, we spent hours talking or playing games around the dining room table. We had a grand time the whole week.

Our hostess had a hummingbird feeder hanging outside her large picture window. From our vantage point behind the glass, we could watch these delicate creatures come and go freely, displaying a variety of brilliant colors. When their long bills were inserted into the tiny cups of the feeder, their graceful bodies were completely suspended in air. As they sipped the sweetened water, their wings moved so fast they were nearly invisible.

A certain brown hummingbird soon caught my attention because he was different from the rest. He was different not only in color but in action. He would perch in a nearby tree, and whenever a bird came for a sweet morsel he dove at it to shoo it away. He was nasty. He gave the other birds no peace. He would not permit them to tarry at the feeding cups.

I soon became quite angry with him when I noticed that he really wasn't drinking and only wanted the feeder for himself. It seemed that his main object was to keep other birds away from the food. I grew crosser and crosser with his selfish behavior as I watched him stir up trouble day after day. I thought, If he doesn't really want the nectar, why can't he at least let the others enjoy the feast?

One evening, shortly after our ranch experience, we were invited to another friend's home for a cup of coffee. During the cool of the evening, we were sitting on their patio in much the same setting as the cabin in which we stayed. This friend also had a bird feeder, which caused me to think of the naughty little brown bird. I related the story of how that little bird had made such a nuisance of himself, making the other birds miserable.

My host then commented that he personally thought God had made brown hummingbirds, better known as Rufous, with that nature for the purpose of keeping other hummingbirds from becoming too dependent on artificial food. Instinctively he was trying to shoo them all away, forcing them to hunt for natural food and keep their wings exercised. Our friend said that Rufous hummingbirds always acted like this because they were born troublemakers. Their bad behavior kept other birds busily searching for natural resources. He said he couldn't prove this theory scientifically but that it made sense to him. I agreed.

After I retired that night, I lay awake thinking about Rufous hummingbirds and what our host had said about them. One thought led to another; I began to see a spiritual correlation. It became evident to me that God has His Rufous' too. He even puts up with unacceptable behavior from them at times because their actions are for the good of others. God permits trouble among His saints for the purpose of strengthening the spiritual prayer wings of other believers who are then driven to the source of real spiritual nourishment.

A few human Rufous hummingbirds actually came to mind that night. I could think of assemblies that had at least one. I could think of families who had a Rufous, too. Some people have a way of keeping things stirred up and making life miserable for others. I'm quite sure they are not aware of being troublemakers. They are merely giving in to the instincts of their old natures. God seems to permit such actions because He knows that in the long run His children will learn to rely on the true source of spiritual food. He wants them to keep their prayer wings in trim. I am aware that I have lost time and energy when I fought back at the human brown hummingbird instead of searching for the Christian's natural food—the Word of God.

The story of David and Shimei, one of his followers, perfectly illustrates this principle (2 Sam. 16:5-15). When David was rejected as king and fled for his life, Shimei threw stones and cursed him. David did not retaliate. He went to God directly for encouragement instead. By deepening his already tremendous faith, he was able to control his mind. Rather than dwelling on Shimei's misdemeanor, David focused on the power of God and it enriched his life. He said in confidence, *"It may be that the Lord will look on mine affliction, and that the Lord will requite me good for his cursing this day"* (2 Sam. 16:12).

David fixed his thoughts on God and not on the problem. Neither did he toy with solutions, which freed God to work on his behalf. God did turn Shimei's cursings into good. We would all be happier and the end results would be exceptionally sweet if we entertained no bitter aftertaste of revenge. We could be spared having to make apologies and our attitudes would be better if we followed Paul's advice, *"Be not overcome of evil, but overcome evil with good"* (Rom. 12:21).

36
Run, and Don't Look Back

When two men arrived from nowhere, Lot invited them to spend the night. It turned out to be quite an experience, unbelievably horrid to say the least (see Gen. 19:1-26). Nerves were already frayed from a long night of debauchery outside the walls of the home. The next morning, the visitors blurted out the news of imminent doom, telling Lot's family to leave Sodom immediately because God was going to completely destroy the city because of its sin.

Surprised and distressed at the men's message, the family found it difficult to conceive of such a thing. There was no evidence of apparent disaster. Lot's wife had a particularly hard time leaving because she liked Sodom, and her family had a history of moving. First they had gone into Egypt with Lot's uncle, Abraham. Shortly after their return, a family quarrel resulted in the division of land between themselves and Abraham's family, necessitating another move. Then there were at least two more moves due to war. Now, at long last, the family was settled into a normal life. Lot had worked his way up into a socially respectable position, and his wife had probably developed friendships that accompanied their prosperous lifestyle. Besides, all her children were nearby. Life was good.

She more than likely questioned the wisdom of following two strangers in the first place, doubting their authority. But since her husband respected them and received what they had said as from the living God, she reluctantly prepared to leave. She dilly-dallied around, but at least started out with

133

the others. Perhaps the sorrow of leaving their married children, who had laughed at the idea of escaping, caused her to have second thoughts. Hesitating to leave friends and family, she allowed the thought of them to pull her back toward Sodom. Ignoring the command, *"Look not behind thee,"* she stopped, turned around to look back toward Sodom, and instantly became a pillar of salt.

The Bible records other stories of people who started out well in their search for deliverance, but later, counting the cost to be too great, gave up. The rich young ruler in Matthew 19:16-22 comes readily to mind. Many of us know people in our modern day who show promise of salvation. Yet somewhere along the line, when they stop to count the cost, they find the price too high.

Our daily newspapers remind us that our Lord's return is very close. Christ said that circumstances in the world would be similar to those of Sodom just before its destruction. Little do people today realize that the cost of not finding eternal life is far, far greater than any price they may have to pay to flee from the destruction of this world. Absolutely nothing in this life is worthy of the loss of eternity with Christ. If we could only give people one glimpse of the Father's house, they would find that it is not to be compared with even their greatest expectations for anything here on earth—possessions, people, pleasure, or prestige. To any people who are pausing to consider the cost, I would say, *"Remember Lot's wife."*

37
SHARE FARMING

A number of years ago, my husband and I read an amusing article in *Reader's Digest* entitled "Beautiful Thieves." Admittedly, it was exaggerated. The author told in a delightfully humorous way how his daughters constantly borrowed his things and seldom returned them. When they did give his things back, they were often in an unusable condition. He referred to his girls as "beautiful, sweet, and clever in their way of borrowing," but added, "Wasn't taking things and using them without permission the same as stealing, especially when they were not returned?"

At the time, we vividly related to what the author wrote because we were having the same problem with three teenagers in our family. We often had a good laugh whenever anything disappeared, because we referred to our daughters as our "beautiful thieves," automatically assuming they were the culprits.

The article came to mind again when I read Malachi 3:8, where God accused the Israelites of stealing from Him. They were flabbergasted and puzzled by what He could possibly mean. They were not aware that they were robbing God, yet He explained that they had failed to return His rightful portion, which He—the Creator and Owner of everything in heaven and earth—had expected them to give.

In reading further, the word "storehouse" appeared, which reminded me of the farmers I had known during my younger years. We lived in a community comprised largely of share farmers. Instead of paying rent for their farms, they shared the crops. The use of the farmhouse and barns was paid for by their labor. That way, in years when the crops were lean, the landowners suffered equally with the farmers. As a whole, this plan worked well.

Some farmers, when they first moved in, were very thankful for the good roof over their heads and food on the table, so they were highly motivated to work hard and long. They were thankful they had to make no outlay of money and were more than happy to share the profit when harvest came. But as years passed, they gradually found it harder to hand over income from the harvest to the owners who had not worked for their share. Human nature being what it is, they soon forgot that the land they farmed did not belong to them. I can remember hearing some grumbling about the landowner's seeming greediness, and a few found ways to wrongly hold back the landowner's share of the profits, especially during tough economic times. I also recall some heated arguments and bits of gossip. Without doubt, there were cases when such complaints were justified.

The Lord's accusation against the Israelites in Malachi 3:8 was perfectly true because He had not been unfair in any sense of the word. *"Will a man rob God? Yet ye have robbed Me,"* God accused. He went on to say, *"But ye say, Wherein have we robbed Thee? In tithes and offerings."* Everything the Israelites (and all mankind) had, belonged to God: health, homes, money, and family. He only asked for a small portion to be returned to Him, yet they failed to comply. In this respect, they were stealing from God, were they not? He certainly reminded them of it.

It's easy for Christians to permit this same situation to happen. The same type of rationalization creeps in. At first, right after salvation, nothing seems too great a sacrifice to make for Christ. It is easy enough at that time to freely work long, hard hours, knowing that everything belongs to Him, and admitting that He has a rightful claim. We are happy to have a safe spiritual umbrella over our heads, and we gladly accept all His provisions, knowing we have nothing. But as the years pass, Satan brings dissatisfaction and makes us think we have certain rights. These tempt us to hold back time, strength, and money. I was challenged, too, by God's accusations, and realized that after the spiritual crops are harvested I will be required to stand before my Creator—the Owner of the great harvest field—to give an account of my labor and explain if I have not been consistent in giving God His just dues.

38
SMALL BEGINNINGS

It is awesome to recall what God accomplished since we purchased a home in 1951 and started our missionary work in Japan. I write with a real sense of reverence, for I am aware that it was God who moved people, controlled economics, and built and is still building His Church in Gumma province.

After completing two years of language school, we needed living quarters for our little family of three young daughters. The city of Takasaki had been laid heavily on Gifford's heart. I can see him still, standing with bowed head on the top of a hill overlooking Takasaki, praying that Christ would build His Church with Christians from that city. At the time of his prayer, we did not know of one local Christian who would help us and we had no home or church building. Rented homes were impossible to find, since the whole area surrounding the city had been leveled by war because of the abundance of war factories in the area. We looked for weeks before we found an available plot of land just outside the city.

The house we found was not worth much because it was old and dilapidated, but it had a gorgeous Japanese garden and, by Japanese standards, was a large piece of property. This one little house had withstood the ravages of war. The house and garden consisted of four lots that had to be purchased as one package. To make the story of years fit on just a couple of pages, I'll say that we bought the land and settled in with our family.

We soon invited our neighbors to join us for Bible studies

with an emphasis in the gospel. At the same time, Gifford rented rooms in various public buildings near three high schools, a university and a college in which he started Bible classes for students. From that beginning, God started a work for Himself. Two or three years later, it was a joyous occasion when we held our first official church services in our living room with five brand new believers from the Bible classes.

Thinking back, step by step, God multiplied the purchase of the land like the loaves and fish in the New Testament. We prayed for years that God would enable us to begin a youth camp work, little realizing we were living on His provision for the camp. Approximately six years after we purchased our house, a gentleman stopped by, and, out of the blue, offered to buy one of the lots. Interestingly enough, within three days another man asked to buy a lot on the opposite side of the house. At the same time, we received a letter from the United States Army offering old barracks to any missionary who would dismantle them and cart them away. All three of these unusual circumstances convinced us that this was God's answer to our prayers about starting a camp and that He was showing us how He would provide the finances and the materials needed for the buildings to make it possible.

After the camp was built, the Bible classes fed into the camp work and the camp work helped the church to grow. The church started to grow until we felt the need of a more suitable, permanent place to worship. The believers, all young people and still young in their faith, united to build a chapel with the help of another young missionary.

Many fruitful years passed until in 1972 we returned to Japan after receiving the prognosis that Gifford's cancer was terminal. He was determined to see his dream of a Christian bookstore built before his death. We saw the Lord stretch and multiply the use of the land one more time. A Christian bookstore was built on part of our land and it was opened October 31, 1974.

After Gifford's death, God multiplied the use of the land once more and a beautiful new chapel replaced our old home on the remaining land and a new home was purchased for me. With the careful planning of a Christian architect in our assembly, the new chapel has ten times the space as the original chapel.

There is one joy even greater than buildings and projects. It is the joy of seeing and feeling the evidence of Christ building His Church through "living stones" which shall never grow old or perish. Praise the Lord, there are now seven churches that have grown out of the tiny little group of believers who first met in our living room. God greatly multiplied the land and the saints for His glory.

39
SPIRITUAL CANNIBALS

The night I was reading a passage in Numbers, I had a severe case of the blues. Thus preoccupied, I was getting little out of my reading:

> *And they went and came to Moses...And they told him and said, we came into the land whither thou sentest us, and surely it floweth with milk and honey; and this is the fruit of it. Nevertheless...there we saw the giants, the sons of Anak, which came of the giants; and we were in our own sight as grasshoppers, and so we were in their sight.*
>
> (Num. 13:26-28, 33)

I read on with a "so what" attitude until the sentence, *"they are bread for us,"* suddenly caught my eye (Num. 14:9). I wondered how people could be bread for the Israelites? I read the verse again to try to get the connection, wondering why people were to become food. If the Israelites ate people as bread, that would make them cannibals, wouldn't it? So I thought.

Sure enough, the very giants themselves, whose size had frightened and discouraged the Israelite spies were to be bread for God's people. *"If the Lord delight in us, then He will bring us into this land, and give it us; a land which floweth with milk and honey. Only rebel not ye against the Lord, neither fear ye the people of the land; for they are bread for us: their defense is departed from them, and the Lord is with us: fear them not"* (Num. 14:8-9).

The humorous idea of the Israelites, who by comparison were like grasshoppers, devouring the giants and the sons of

Anak struck me as being funny and nursed me through my hurts, lifting my spirits. I knew, of course, the meaning was not to be taken literally.

Before I knew it, it was morning. When I awoke, I was still chuckling to myself.

All that next day, the same train of thought followed me. Bit by bit, snatches of messages I'd heard on this passage made the meaning clearer. The more I pondered, the more I could identify with the Israelites as I began to recognize the spiritual giants in my life. It became obvious that if I did not devour the giants first, they would devour me. *"Have all the workers of iniquity no knowledge? who eat up My people as they eat bread, and call not upon the Lord"* (Ps. 14:4).

I hate facing giants. However, it became apparent that if I allowed fear of them to keep me from entering the Promised Land, which flowed with perfect peace and rest, I would actually be rebelling against God. Fear stems from unbelief. It is just as serious an offense to refuse to claim His promises and to trust Him to go before us today as it was for the Israelites to refuse to enter Canaan.

Admittedly, the giants are huge and their offspring are many, but they all descend from one father. Just as God promised the Israelites that He would go before them and drive out the giants, so God promises to drive out the spiritual giants before me. My responsibility is to arrange my forces for battle, put on the whole armor of God, and to stand against the giants even though I am no more a match for these giants than grasshoppers were against the sons of Anak.

Identifying the giants and their descendants is my first step in defeating them. Matching the piece of armor to the sin from which it can protect me is also of utmost importance as I advance. I must capture and conquer the Anaks of pride, prejudice, envy, grudging, fear and the like. I must be ruthless with these scoundrels and chew them up. I need to consume them as bread. When I do so, they become food and nourishment that give me spiritual strength.

The older I get, the bigger some giants seem to grow, especially when I let myself shrivel up spiritually. The more gigantic my need for security, comfort, avoiding conflict, stress, and loneliness becomes, the more it is necessary to stand against them. By doing so I actually become stronger for having encountered them. They actually become food to me.

40
STANDING BRAVELY

I've tried to imagine what the woman whose story is told in John 8:1-11 was thinking about when she saw Jesus stoop down and begin writing in the sand. With her heart pounding, she knew that she was guilty of the sin of which she had been accused. After all, she had been caught in the act. According to Jewish law, she was supposed to die. Considering the number and status of her accusers, there was no use defending herself. She cringed as she expected the first stone to hit her.

I also wonder what Jesus wrote. You may wonder, too, but there is no doubt why John didn't include that piece of information. In that way the message is relevant to each individual at the appropriate time. It is necessarily different to each of us, according to our need for forgiveness at each particular time. No matter what Christ wrote, He got His point across. It pricked the consciences of everyone present. They began to leave the Lord's presence, one by one.

However, I believe the woman was the only one really convicted to the extent that, even before Christ told her not to sin again, she decided to turn her life around. At that moment, she made a decision that not only changed her lifestyle but affected her eternal future. She decided to remain where she stood, in Christ's presence, to face the guilt instead of running from it as the others had. The "fruit of repentance" soon produced the fruit of righteousness.

While the scribes and Pharisees who had brought her were leaving, she had the opportunity to slip out, too.

Christ was looking down, deep in thought and occupied with what He was writing in the sand. He did not even look at her. The scribes and Pharisees left because their consciences bothered them, but she stayed for exactly the same reason. Her conscience bothered her, too, and she wasn't any more comfortable then they, but she did not want to leave His presence carrying her guilt with her. She didn't offer excuses by shifting blame to the man who was as guilty as she was; she only wanted relief from the awful weight of her sin.

When Christ finally addressed her again, He was direct and to the point. He spoke of sin, not excusing hers, but he freely forgave her and warned her not to commit this sin again. With that proclamation, she was not only free from sin but was free to leave lighthearted; she had been exonerated. The same presence of the Son of God that sent the scribes and Pharisees running from Him warmed and purified her heart as she bravely stood in His presence.

Not too long after this, perhaps with this incident in mind, Christ declared Himself to be the light of the world (John 8:12). He may have thought of the Pharisees who scampered for cover when the light of God uncovered the filth in their hearts.

Whenever I read this story, I am reminded of the time I lifted a sizable flat stone in my garden. As you may know, Japan is a damp country, so insects are plentiful. As soon as the sunlight hit the ground where the stone had been, it seemed that thousands of bugs scampered for cover. In the same way that sunlight sends insects scampering, Jesus' holy presence sent the scribes and Pharisees fleeing from exposure of their sins. At the same time, the light of His presence shone into the woman's heart, purified her, and gave her new life.

One evening, in an English Bible class, a student told an amusing yet sobering true story that had happened at work. He was employed in a company that prepared and packaged lunches. A young lady, being hungry, took one of the lunches and went to (what she thought was) an unused, secluded room to eat it. As soon as she had finished the meal, she heard her name called over the loudspeaker, asking her to come to the front office. There she faced a group of executives, who told her they had watched her devour the lunch on video. (She had been completely oblivious to a video camera in a corner of the room.) To her, taking a lunch was a small offense, but in the eyes of these men it was stealing that needed to be nipped in the bud. They merely reprimanded her, made her pay for the lunch, and strongly warned her not to let it happen again. I'll let you imagine what her embarrassment was like!

In the same manner, Christ reprimanded the adulterous woman and warned her to sin no more. Praise His precious name! When we choose to stand firm in Christ's light, seeing our sin as He sees our sin, we are purified. It is not easy to stand bravely in the exposure of His light. By taking responsibility for our sins, we, too, can experience the blessedness of perfect forgiveness from the God of this universe. We, too, can walk away lighthearted with a spring in our step to face a new life absolutely free of guilt. Oh, the joy of knowing that we are new creatures in Christ Jesus!

41
TAKE IT BY THE TAIL

Reading Moses's story in Exodus 4:1-5 brought back to mind an incident that occurred while we were getting our camp in shape one spring. Several of us were busy pulling weeds out of a retaining wall when suddenly the young man working closest to me shrieked. Jumping back in fright, he realized that the big weed he had reached out to pull was a snake with its head sticking out from between the stones and its tongue flicking in danger. It was a shocking experience to both of us. Although it turned out to be a harmless snake, snakes are still snakes! I could feel the same repulsive reaction that Moses felt in the incident related in Exodus 4.

God had ordered Moses to fling his rod down, and as he did so it became a serpent. Moses jumped back, too, like the boy and I did that day at camp. He even started to run away, but God stopped him in his tracks and did not permit him to continue running. Moses' terrified reaction in seeing his familiar rod suddenly become a snake is understandable, but God called him back and clearly told him to pick up the repulsive creature—by its tail.

As frightening an experience as this was, Moses did exactly as God commanded him to do, and when he did, the snake turned back into a rod.

Until this point, Moses had been living a quiet life as a shepherd in the country on the west side of the desert, but God had many lessons for him to learn. Moses was about to start off on an important mission of delivering God's people from Egypt. Knowing that Moses trusted too much in the comfort and security of his shepherd's rod, God wanted him to transfer that feeling of trust onto Him alone. God gave him very clear confirmation of His power. He said that He was sending him forth and promised to be with him constantly.

Moses' experience also reminded me of the year we were building Ikaho Bible Camp. Our experience could hardly be compared to Moses' picking up a snake, but I saw a parallel. We had deliberated for three years while looking for suitable land and seeking assurance that God wanted us to go ahead. The way seemed to open before us when we were able to buy land in the foothills. Carpenters were already transforming three used army barracks into dormitories when Gifford suddenly collapsed.

Everything went topsy-turvy. Gifford was hospitalized with bleeding ulcers, and as a result we ran out of money. At the same time, opposition to the camp came from a very unexpected source. There were other complications as well, but I will spare you those details.

I was just as frightened by the sudden turn of events as Moses was. My first reaction was to run away (and to let the snake run away, too), but I thank God today that He did not let me. A few months passed before we witnessed the miracle of God's changing our serpent back into a rod by healing Gifford and supplying the needs for the camp. I know now the tremendous blessing we would have missed if we had run. Instead, we saw the Lord bring thousands of young people through the camp during the thirty years of its operation. The joy of seeing people born into God's family and the witnessing of decisions made to follow Christ more than compensated for the unpleasant experience and unwanted doubts that accompanied the camp's beginning.

Moses needed God's confirmation before he started out on his mission because not too long afterward he ran into opposition. At first the Israelites received the news that they were going to be delivered with great rejoicing, and they gladly worshiped God. However, when things suddenly went into reverse and Pharaoh's behavior drastically changed, the people turned against Moses and blamed him. Pharaoh unjustly added new burdens to their lives, and the people became so angry with Moses that at times they even talked of stoning him. Then Moses needed to look back to the experience in the desert and remember God's confirmation that He would be with him.

I'm sure we have all had situations when, after we've started some service for the Lord, it seems to go all wrong and becomes as threatening to us as picking up a serpent. Many have started teaching Sunday school, using their homes for Bible study groups, or discipling individuals, but something happens to spoil the effort. This can be in the form of humiliating experiences, personality clashes, cruel criticism, or misunderstanding. The number of things that can become serpent-like are numerous. Rather than being surprised by such situations, we should think of Moses. We should be encouraged and, like Moses, stoop to pick up our serpent and fully expect God to turn it into a rod. God often permits unpleasant experiences to prove that He is with us and can work out all things in His time.

42
THE DO-IT-FOR-ME COMPLEX

We live in an age in which many people have the incurable disease I call the Do-it-for-me complex, and unless there is a divine touch of Christ's healing hand, in extreme cases the disease is terminal. There are ways for us to keep its symptoms under control and to suppress their effects, but the only lasting antidote is therapy through the blood of Christ. Christ's blood needs to be applied not only at the time of salvation but whenever the disease flares up again. This illness did not begin in this generation, however. Two very dear men of God contracted a severe case of it nearly two thousand years ago, and mankind has actually had this disease since the days of Adam.

Let's look back to when Christ had just shared with His disciples the suffering and agony that lay ahead of Him. James and John were so occupied with their own thoughts that they failed to take in the real meaning and the cost for Christ. They were making their own plans and had big hopes for the future.

I am surprised that when Christ was facing the cross they made the request to Him: *"We would that Thou shouldest do for us whatsoever we shall desire"* (Mark 10:35). I am amazed at their insensitivity to how He was feeling at the time. It is hard to imagine they could have been so selfish. But then I thought: Wait a minute, Madge. How long has it been since you have evaluated your own thoughts and analyzed your own prayer requests? I finally had to admit that I had a fair case of the disease myself.

From this passage, my mind went on to the older brother of the prodigal son described in Luke 15:25-32. I saw a similar attitude in this boy, who was so preoccupied with his own thoughts that he couldn't share the joy of his father when the younger brother returned home. He was eaten up with jealousy when he saw the royal welcome the prodigal received from his father.

The seeming injustice of such quick forgiveness was more than he could take. No doubt the harsh words said when the younger son left home flooded into his mind. By comparison, he felt he deserved more than his "bad boy" brother did. These normal thoughts caused him to be self-centered, which in turn resulted in such self-pity that he wanted no part in the celebration. He remembered only his long, tedious hours of work on the farm while his brother partied and spent his father's money. Occupied with what he had done and what he thought he deserved from his father as a reward, the older son completely forgot the blessings he had received and that the very land he tilled was his father's—a normal reaction to a Do-it-for-me Complex.

I'm also reminded of a present-day story of a friend of mine who, as a young boy, was with his father near a lake when the cry came that a girl was drowning. His father jumped in and saved the child's life, but in doing so caught severe pneumonia that took his life a few days later. Unbelievably, the family of the little girl never came back to thank him because, evidently, moving away was more acceptable than helping his widowed mother and her three small children.

Christ, facing the cross, was heavy with anticipating the burden of sin. James and John added to His grief by showing just how little of the meaning of the Cross they had grasped. Their request to be with Christ was a good one, but they failed to see that Christ would not personally rule in His Kingdom for quite a while.

The older brother robbed the father of his full share of the joy in the return of his beloved son by refusing to join with the others during the happy celebration. The family added to the sorrow of the devastated widow and children in their loss by their lack of sympathy and gratefulness.

What a lovely contrast we have in Jonathan (see 1 Sam. 20). He knew that David would replace him on the throne, yet we read in 1 Samuel 20:34, *"Jonathan...was grieved for David, because his father had done him shame."* Jonathan was not thinking of himself; he was thinking only of the wrong done to David.

I have been encouraged through seeing a similar contrast in the friend I referred to. I have watched his reactions since he was in high school. Anger and bitterness, triggered through self-pity, played a large part in his life until he received Christ as His Saviour in a Bible class. He learned almost simultaneously to forgive and forget. He truly became a new person in Christ Jesus. Instead of thinking only of asking the Lord to fulfill his desires and to make up to him what he had missed in the loss of his father, he began to serve the Lord wholeheartedly. Today the results of this decision are evident in his life. The Lord has blessed him with a lovely wife and two precious children. We know that Christ will reign and one day we will reign with Him as we enter the joy of the Father. Therefore, the sooner we can replace our Do-it-for-me Complex with a Do-it-for-Christ attitude, the better.

43
THE QUEEN OF SHEBA

Something prompted the Queen of Sheba to make a tremendously long journey to Jerusalem. Whatever it was, she felt it worthwhile to pay a great price in both time and money. The journey meant leaving important political duties. The hot, grueling hours of a two-thousand-mile trek in those days would have made any woman think twice before setting out on such a colossal undertaking. I'm sure the discomfort of the trip made her think that she would bake alive in her chariot.

Many years later, the Lord held her up as an example of diligent sacrifice (Matt. 12:42) when He retold her story in order to challenge people to seek to know Him and to really see His glory. He said that she made the trip to hear the wisdom of Solomon. She had heard about him and wanted to see for herself if what she had heard was true. 1 Kings 10:2-5 tells us, *"And when she was come to Solomon, she communed with him of all that was in her heart. And Solomon told her all her questions: there was not anything hid from the king, which he told her not. And when the Queen of Sheba had seen all Solomon's wisdom...there was no more spirit in her."*

All the glory of his kingdom certainly impressed her: his planning, his provision for his household, and his court. The more she saw, the more she wanted to see. There was no end to her questions, and she was overwhelmed by his answers. They far surpassed all she had imagined. The tedious trip seemed trivial in comparison to the reward of gaining an inside view of his great empire. He had answered life's basic questions for her and she was satisfied.

The Lord said of her, *"The queen of the south shall rise up in the judgment with this generation, and shall condemn it: for she came from the uttermost parts of the earth to hear the wisdom of Solomon; and, behold, a greater than Solomon is here"* (Matt. 12:42). Christ acknowledged that the trip had cost her much. But He as much as said that if she was willing to pay that great homage to another human being, how much greater a sacrifice the people of His generation should have been willing to make to hear His wisdom. He intimated that people will be judged for their lack of interest in seeking the wisdom of the one "greater than Solomon." Since I met Christ personally, I wonder how much of my time and effort I have willingly sacrificed in seeking His glory and receiving His answers to life's questions. At times it seems so much easier to seek the thoughts of men and to seek their honor than to seek the wisdom of Christ.

Recently, Isaiah 6:3 took on new meaning for me. I noticed that it didn't say heaven is full of the Lord's glory but rather that *"the whole earth is full of His glory."*

During the two or three days I have been meditating on the fullness of the earth's glory, a family of robins, growing brave because of the protection of the windowpane, built a nest and started their family just outside my kitchen window. It has been an interesting firsthand nature study.

The closer I have watched, the more I have become aware of God's great wisdom in His perfect creation and sensed what it means to see His glory on this earth. I marveled at the instinct of these lovely creatures as they built their nest. After the young hatched, both parents were kept busy feeding their family. It was amazing to see how gently the mother coaxed the young up out of the nest onto a branch. After they fluttered to the ground, she immediately taught them to scratch for food. She was a wise, protective, and patient parent. Just thinking of God's marvelous wisdom and His power in creation assures me that He has all the answers to life's puzzling questions and that it is His purpose for me to make sacrifices in seeking to enjoy and become more aware of His power and glory.

I highly doubt that the Queen of Sheba used her experience to merely satisfy her intellectual curiosity. Rather, her personal life and political reign had a far-reaching effect after she had been changed by what she saw. Many other people profited from the sacrifice she made. Just thinking about her challenges me. I pray for a consuming desire to see the glory of Christ while I'm still on this earth so that when I meet my "Greater than Solomon," the Queen of Sheba will have no occasion to rise up as a witness to my indifference.

44
THE TONGUE—TAIL OF THE HEART

An African proverb says that the tongue is the tail of the heart and that it wags to the tune of the heart. If Job's wife's tongue was wagging to the tune of her heart, we have a pretty sad picture of her internal condition. She was in a shocking state of despair when she said, *"Dost thou still retain thine integrity? Curse God, and die"* (Job 2:9). Can you imagine any woman encouraging her husband to die, no matter how disappointed she may have been?

Michal's tongue also expressed the jealousy she harbored in her heart when she said to David in sarcasm, *"How glorious was the king of Israel today"* (2 Sam. 6:16, 20). It would seem that she just couldn't stand to see his joy and rapture at seeing the ark of the Lord brought back into Jerusalem. Evidently she was envious of his devotion to the Lord and his interest in the Lord's concerns. She, too, revealed what was on the inside through the wagging of her tongue.

Linking the tongue with the heart is not a new idea. David was aware of the tongue's power and he knew well that the emotion of the heart set the tongue in motion. He prayed, *"Let the words of my mouth, and the meditation of my heart, be acceptable in Thy sight, O Lord"* (Ps. 19:14). I realize now how often in the past I have been deceived into thinking that what I said was absolutely correct when in reality it wasn't correct at all. Because my heart was deceived, I said cruel things out of envy and jealousy, thus hurting people although not purposefully meaning to do so.

I'm reminded of a game my friends and I often played as

teenagers. We would build houses from matches, with each person adding a match in turn. The taller the house got, the longer we held our breath as each of us tried to add one more match without making the whole structure tumble down. One false move and everything collapsed. In the same way, people are crushed, homes are toppled, and churches are destroyed by one last, biting remark when people give vent to their thoughts through their tongues. Only God knows the number of hearts that have been broken, lives that have been damaged, and homes and churches that have been split by words expressed by angry persons.

It has been said that "jealousy is the little soul's grouch at seeing its own rejected ideals realized in another." "Envy," someone else said, "is the unwilling respect that inferiority pays to superiority." Both of these sayings affirm the truth that the problem lies in the heart and not the tongue. It's the heart that is deceived by Satan's lies. Thus the only way to prevent damage through the tongue is to cure the heart.

Job's wife would have encouraged him if she had returned to the truth of God's sovereignty. If she had accepted what God brought into their lives as well as Job did, she would have helped him instead of suggesting that he end it all. She was not the comfort and help he badly needed. Rather, she encouraged him to turn his back on God.

Michal also would have been much happier if she had shared her husband's worship and joy in the Lord while he was leading the celebration instead of being embarrassed and angry at him. She would have been delighted that the Lord had been glorified when the ark was brought back to its rightful place in Jerusalem if her heart had been right before Him.

How easily I am deceived by Satan into thinking that I am being mistreated when actually I feel jealousy, envy, or anger at a person who has tremendous joy in the Lord. Knowing this helps me to understand that other people often have the same problem. Being conscious that others can be afflicted with the same malady lets me accept the negative things they say without being hurt personally. Paul exhorts us to keep our minds (hearts) girded with truth at all times. Instead of expressing all that comes to mind, as Job's friends did, I would do well to seriously question if my impressions are the truth and if the other person's perceptions are also the truth. In this way, by keeping my heart and mouth truthful and joyful, the wagging of my tongue that is merely the tail of my heart will be better controlled, less hurtful to others, and much more beneficial.

45
THE TRUTH SHALL MAKE YOU FREE

I seldom read the story in Luke 13:11-13 about the woman who was bent double for eighteen years without thinking of my dear grandmother, who also was bent over like the woman Luke mentions. Grandma, a farmer's wife, had worked hard in the fields all her life. I remember seeing her grimace in pain as she tried to straighten up. The process of spinal deterioration was slow, and as the years passed it became more and more difficult for her to stand straight. Finally the day came when it was too much of an effort to try. Both of these women suffered from a physical disease that kept them looking down and bound to themselves. It was a miserable existence.

The woman Luke mentions met Christ one day in one of the synagogues. When He stretched out His hands, His loving touch healed her and released her from her bondage to herself so she was able to stand straight again. This was a miracle, because until that day her bones had fused together. She must have experienced pure joy to be able to look people in the face once again. She praised God for the relief from pain and for being able to move about freely. After looking at her feet for eighteen years, she realized how wonderful it was to have normal movement—something so many of us take for granted. How precious this freedom was to her!

In John 8, Christ tells us about another disease that brings a person into bondage. The disease of sin brings spiritual bondage, bondage to ourselves caused by degeneration of the spiritual spine. Christ said, *"Whosoever committeth sin is the servant of sin"* (John 8:34). The result of spiritual bondage is also grievously painful and real because it cripples and disables people.

Any sin has the power to bring a person into bondage, but I think the most common sin which results in an emotional binding to oneself is the sin of self-pity and self-occupation, usually caused by unresolved anger and bitterness. Release from this debilitation is as great a miracle as we see in the story in Luke's Gospel. Only our Lord and Saviour, Jesus Christ, can give us perfect release from ourself and provide permanent healing. Jesus said, *"If the Son therefore, shall make you free, ye shall be free indeed"* (John 8:36).

Sin has a thousand ways to keep us bound to ourselves in different degrees. A person can measure the extent of the damage by making a catalogue of his or her thoughts for one week. One of the psalmists said, *"God is not in all his thoughts"* (Ps. 10:4). There was no room for God in their thoughts because they were too occupied with themselves. When Satan approached Eve in the Garden of Eden, we recall he first captured her thoughts by making her think of herself. Causing her to be dissatisfied with her ignorance and enticing her to gain more wisdom by eating from the Tree of the Knowledge of Good and Evil, he created within her the desire to become like God.

Worry, fear, disobedience, jealousy, vengefulness, criticism, suspicion, self-justification and even laziness make us think about ourselves. Before we know it, we find that it becomes increasingly difficult to stand straight emotionally and spiritually. Despondency, disillusionment and fear soon follow suit. There are various degrees, but every human being suffers from it in one form or another.

As for me, I've had to go to Christ countless times when feeling the influence of any of the things mentioned above and ask for a touch of His hand. It has been my experience that His healing touch always comes through His Word.

Christ said in John 8:32, *"Ye shall know the truth, and the truth shall make you free."*

At the time of salvation, sad to say, not all the symptoms of sin are eradicated, though the root of sin is dealt with by the blood of Christ. Whether instantly or slowly, it is a miracle when Christ frees us from preoccupation with ourselves.

Paul also carried on the same thought in Ephesians 6:14 when he told the believers they must constantly have the loins (the strength which allows us to stand) of their minds girded about with truth. It is the truth about ourselves and the truth about Jesus Christ which frees us from our malady and makes it possible for us to stand tall before God and man.

46

THE WOMAN'S PLACE IN THE HOME

When Christ wanted to teach us about His relationship with the Church, He illustrated His precious truths through the home—the most common institution possible, the ordinary place with which we are all so familiar (Eph. 5:22-30). What a tremendous thought dressed in such ordinary language!

Because the home is a sacred example before the world, Paul gave his instructions regarding the home carefully. Through Titus, for example, Paul gave explicit instructions to young women concerning their responsibilities in their homes. What he wrote centuries ago is just as important for us today: *"Teach the young women to be sober, to love their husbands, to love their children, to be discreet, chaste, keepers at home, good, obedient to their own husbands, that the word of God be not blasphemed"* (Titus 2: 4-5). It is important that the Christian home be a place of love, orderliness, obedience, and godliness. In the home, God is either exalted or blasphemed. The achievement of orderliness and obedience falls primarily on the woman if she is running her home on biblical principles. She contributes much to the family in those areas.

Christ is love. Consequently, when Christ is the center of the home, it will pivot around love, which is patient, kind, loyal, and creates a warm atmosphere of happy fellowship. Children, for example learn love and respect from watching their mother and following her good example. The more a woman tries to exemplify Christ, the more that envy, jealousy, boasting, pride, selfishness, rudeness, touchiness, grudges, and injustice will be discouraged. This may seem to be impossible at times, but at least she can work toward this goal.

When Paul admonished young women to be keepers at home, he was stressing how important it was for women to nurture order, peace, and rest in their homes. A home without these characteristics soon becomes a place of confusion and chaos, which is a direct result of our sinful natures and a reminder to all of the fall of man. I realize that for a woman with young children this is a tall order, but there are ways to maintain orderliness even with toys strewn about. It is possible to let children have freedom in their own sphere by teaching them how, when, and where the boundaries are. Through practice children then learn where to draw the line.

In thinking back to my childhood, I remember Mother for her great ability to maintain orderliness in our home. Admittedly, this was two generations ago, but the principle is still a good one. Every day of the week had its special responsibilities. To Mother's way of thinking, for example, the Lord's day began on Saturday afternoon. Baking was done, and everything possible was prepared on Saturday in order to make Sunday morning relaxed and smooth. Shoes were polished, and our clothes were laid out—even a fresh handkerchief for everyone. Saturday evening activities were limited. We had to study our Sunday school lessons and learn our memory verses, then we were free to have fun. No rushing or scrambling about was permitted on Sunday morning.

The home is also to be a place of obedience because it is to exemplify the Church's obedience to Christ. In all relationships such as wife to husband, children to parents, and everyone to God, submission is needed in order for God to be honored. It is wonderful to be the recipient of a godly man's love and protection but, sad to say, some men destroy what God intended for the Christian home by taking advantage of their headship. Even under such circumstances, if a wife, for the

Lord's sake, does not demand her own way and is subject as much as possible to the wishes of her husband and family, their home will be a more peaceful place.

It is impossible to measure a woman's influence on her husband, children, relatives, and neighbors. If she has a positive influence, Christ is glorified. If not, Christ and His Word are made to no avail. Do you think it is fair to say that a woman's love for her family can be measured by the sacrifices she is willing to make for them? Imagine the joy that will be hers when Christ rewards her for exalting Him through her home.

47

TRUSTING THE COMFORT OF GOD

The first forty-seven years of my life were pleasant—not perfect, but comfortable. I had a normal childhood, the blessing of marriage to a fine Christian man, and three healthy children. All of these circumstances contributed to a full and happy life. Then, within a matter of months, the great comforts and joys of my life collapsed.

First, my father died. Dad and I had always been close, and until he became ill he wrote to me every week. I really missed his letters because they had been filled with family news as well as encouragement and help. His letters were like a cup of cold water to a thirsty soul, and this encouragement had been especially important to me during the years my husband and I served on the mission field.

The second and even harder blow came when we learned that Gifford had cancer, which necessitated one hospitalization after another. Within a short time, he underwent five major surgeries. This, combined with the departure of my three daughters to the United States to continue their education, caused me to feel as if my life was falling apart at the seams. What made my situation so difficult was that all three of these emotionally shattering events happened close together, and I was helpless to change anything.

During this time, I had to endure long periods of weekly visits to the hospital and waiting for test reports as I watched Gifford slowly deteriorate. My spirits usually matched his changes in physical health as he grew weaker. In spite of the personal hardships, or perhaps because of them, I learned many lessons during those difficult days. It is impossible to put on paper everything the Lord taught me, but let me share three lessons with you.

First and foremost, I learned in a small way what it meant to take God at His Word. One morning, well into Gifford's illness, I was exceptionally discouraged. Many people had joined us in praying for the Lord's healing or at least the easing of his pain, but neither request was answered. In fact, his pain worsened, and God seemed more silent to our pleas. That particular morning when I got out of bed, I glanced up at the familiar hand-painted plaque above my bed that one of our daughters had painted at camp. It read, "Prayer Changes Things." Until that morning, I had prized her gift, but this particular morning the plaque I had so treasured seemed only to mock me. I thought: Prayer has changed nothing! The difficult events have only continued without respite. If anything, they have increased in intensity.

I had a sudden and strong urge to smash that plaque into a thousand pieces, giving vent to the feelings I was afraid to verbalize. After dressing, I headed toward the back door, plaque in hand, determined to break it on the cement walk. But before opening the outside door, I stepped into the storage room. There, I dropped to my knees and with the plaque on the floor in front of me, I began to pray. Starting with my complaints and grievances, I poured out my heart to the Lord, sparing Him nothing as I accused Him of not intervening on our behalf. I gave vent to my doubts and rebellion, which to that point I had denied.

I do not know how long this lasted, but finally a passage of Scripture flashed into my mind. It was Psalms 18:30, *"As for God, His way is perfect."* My reaction to it was, "No, God, Your way is far from perfect." I certainly did not like the way the Lord was treating us at that point. It seemed unfair that He would allow such a faithful servant who had given himself so completely to suffer like this. Then the Holy Spirit showed me that if I questioned what God had said about Himself, I was making Him a liar, and I was afraid to do that.

Until that moment, my inability to accept our situation as being from God caused darkness and confusion, but with the coming of this verse and the thoughts guided by the Spirit of God, I saw the seriousness of my rebellion. This staunched my tears of self-pity, and a quietness actually began to settle over me as I prayed, using the same words a father in New Testament times had prayed: *"Lord, I believe; help Thou mine unbelief"* (Mark 9:24). I still found it impossible to believe that the Lord's ways with us were perfect, but I cried to Him to help me believe.

Within a matter of minutes after this decision and my plea for help, the darkness and confusion gave way to light and peace. I was able to pick up the plaque, walk back into the bedroom, and hang it in its customary place. Looking at it, I realized that God had not changed a solitary *thing*, but He certainly had changed *me* and my reactions. This lesson was a real turning point for me. The miracle of God's work in my heart proved to me that God is alive and that He is a God of His Word. Only God, through the work of the Holy Spirit, can bring calm to a heart in the middle of a storm.

A second valuable lesson I learned during that time was that our faith pleases God. As the writer of Hebrews says, *"Without faith it is impossible to please Him"* (11:6). I learned this lesson painfully as I sat with Gifford and watched him suffer night after night. He had been an untiring servant of the Lord, always presenting the gospel with the same zeal whether he spoke to one person or to hundreds. Although I questioned God's love, Gifford never seemed to do that. If he did, he never voiced it. In fact, the night before he died, I asked him, "How do you feel toward Christ right now? Do you still love Him?"

He answered, "Oh, I never loved Him more."

The smile on his face told me that he had no doubts of

Christ's love for him, even under those circumstances. His perfect assurance of soon seeing Him brightened his face. I knew then that his implicit, unquestioning trust and love— even in the face of death—brought special joy to the Lord. I realized that my husband's unwavering faith in Christ's love and his devotion to Him meant more to God than his previous service. This left me with the strong desire to learn to know God in the same trustful, intimate way.

I learned the third lesson night after long night as we wondered how we would make it until morning. Somehow, with the Lord's help, we always did. I gradually realized that His grace was sufficient moment by moment and that the power of Christ resting upon us, made it possible (2 Cor. 12:9). He did not tempt us more than we could bear but faithfully provided just enough relief to get us through each day. His relief came in numerous forms, such as the volunteer help of excellent missionary nurses, a neighborhood doctor who often stopped by to check on the two of us when he passed our house, lots of good music supplied by our Christian friends, and plenty of support from fellow believers in Japan as well as letters from friends around the world. All of these mercies were unsolicited but gratefully accepted as special gifts from the Lord. His grace was truly sufficient.

God is the Father of mercy and the God of all comfort. He never did heal Gifford's body, but He certainly healed my soul, not once but many times. I can say now with full assurance that not only is His way perfect, but that as I trust Him, He makes my way perfect (Ps. 18:32).

48

WE BURIED A GOD

We were late in getting home from language school. My head felt like a sausage mill, and my body was tired from shopping and fighting rush-hour traffic on the way home. So while waiting for supper to cook, I stretched out on our bed upstairs. It really felt good to lie flat, but, while half dozing in the rapidly darkening room, I was suddenly awakened by a commotion under our bedroom window.

I did not understand half of what was being said. The disturbance of a chorus of loud, angry voices sounded worse perhaps than it really was, but being the coward I am, I was afraid to look out of the window and see what was going on. I held my breath in silence as I tried to catch the topic of the conversation. I caught one word without mistake, *kamisama,* which was repeated again and again. I knew kamisama came from two words: *kami,* the word for god, and *sama* made it honorific, being added to any word to make it especially polite. I knew without doubt that *kamisama* was the cause of the problem.

I was petrified with fear because we had always found our Japanese neighbors to be dignified and courteous, but I could tell by the vehemence with which they spoke that their emotions were definitely stirred. I could think of nothing we had done to make them this angry and was sure we hadn't done anything to offend one of their gods.

At this time we were sharing a duplex with Harry and Ellen Steele, also new missionaries to Japan. I could hear Gifford's and Harry's voices among the chorus of the others'.

They were having a difficult time calming the people down, but finally I caught the fact that they were returning whatever it was we had been accused of stealing and desecrating. Later, at the dinner table, I heard the full story.

I must digress to let you know the background of this incident. There was limited space for six children to play in the yard of the duplex. The situation was made worse by all the laundry that needed to be hung outside by our two families. So the men put their heads together to think of a way to free up space in the yard. They came up with the idea of using a wire clothesline attached to a pulley, which would be mounted on a pole in the corner of the yard, and fed from the upstairs deck. The clothesline would then be high enough that the children could play under it. The pulley had arrived that day, so both men were eager to install it. Anchoring the pole securely into the ground was a problem because it would have to securely hold the weight of many loads of wash.

They gathered stones, dug a hole, and mixed a small amount of cement for the job. That simple act was the beginning of the commotion. A neighbor had noticed that one of the men had gone across the alley to a vacant lot, taken what seemed to be an innocent-looking rock about a foot and a half in length, and dumped the rock into the hole. In reality the rock was considered sacred by the community. It made a perfect prop for the pole as it was cemented into place, but it caused all the fuss because the neighbors wanted to be sure they got their "stolen" rock back before the cement hardened. After the rock was removed and washed, the people quieted down and explained why the rock was so greatly revered.

Many decades ago, a priest from the local temple had relaxed on that rock in the cool of the evening and had prayed that this country area would one day be turned into a thriving town. Since that time the town had incorporated. Feeling that the priest's prayer was answered, the community reverenced the rock as a god. The only people who had not been

180

aware of that were "us" missionaries, who were still new to the country, culture, and neighborhood.

However, our story had a happy ending because it got us acquainted with our neighbors very quickly! They were friendly after our apologies were made, and they saw how willing both men were to resolve the problem and consider their neighbors' feelings. The experience gave us insight into Japanese thinking and the depth of their beliefs, and it made us realize how necessary it was to be covered by the prayers of the Lord's people.

However, it was alarming to see how quickly an innocent misunderstanding can grow and how quickly a situation beyond our control got out of hand. Had our neighbors not been so easily appeased, it could have been the beginning of a very difficult time for us. I strongly encourage you to pray for all missionaries who are in language study and especially those who are adjusting to a new culture that they may have discernment in all matters and be sensitive to the people they are working among.

I highly doubt that even a new missionary has ever been tempted to acquire a stone god with the purpose of worshipping it, but missionaries, as well as all Christians, need to guard against other forms of gods, for they are as susceptible to worshipping idols as anyone else. John felt the subject was important enough to close his letter with the words, *"Keep yourselves from idols"* (1 John 5:21).

The list of false gods is without end, and all of them are insidious. Methodology, talents, pet peeves, health, security, plans, etc.—all have the possibility of becoming gods if we let them. Anything that captures our thoughts and controls our actions may become a god to us, no matter how good or natural it seems. By analyzing our thoughts, we can soon detect false gods. Our first thoughts in the morning, our last thoughts at night, and the thoughts we wake up with in the middle of the night have the possibility of replacing thoughts of God Himself. *"Ye turned to God from idols to serve the living and true God; and to wait for His Son from heaven..."* (1 Thess. 1:9, 10).

49
WHAT PLEASES CHRIST MOST

Luke tells us that Martha had invited the Lord into their family home and had treated Him as a very important guest (Luke 10:38-42). She planned a delicious, attractive meal and began working on it early, hoping to please Christ and His followers with the very best she could provide. Without a shadow of doubt, Jesus held a prominent place in Martha's heart and home.

Her sister Mary was also pleased when she heard that the Lord was coming to visit, for she dearly loved Him and greatly anticipated talking with Him. She knew He had the answers to all of life's problems. Instead of thinking about what to serve Him, she was far more interested in the spiritual food He would serve her.

To Mary, time spent with Christ was never boring. She loved to sit at His feet and ask many questions about future events, heaven, eternal life, and Him. Hearing His answers was interesting, beneficial, and uplifting, but Luke did not record their conversation for us. I like to imagine that Luke wanted us to have the joy of asking our own questions and receiving answers for ourselves from His written Word. One thing Luke makes clear is that Mary had an intimate relationship with Christ. Being eager to listen, she received satisfactory answers. Jesus was not only a prominent Guest in their home but to Mary was preeminent.

I can sympathize with both Mary and Martha. Mary, from her heart of love, wanted to be with Christ; yet Martha was not out of line in the least when she asked Mary for help. The longer it took for Mary to come to her assistance, the more irritated Martha became. Finally, in desperation, she approached the Lord in a grumbling attitude and complained about Mary's lack of help.

There have been times when, like Martha, I have complained about being overworked and asked the Lord to send someone to come to my assistance. I wanted to use Him as a sounding board, hoping He would magically cure all the family and church injustices. It always seems so much easier to talk to Him rather than to listen to what He has to say to me.

Mary, however, did not allow herself to be distracted at that particular time by household duties. She had made a deliberate choice to give Christ the priority, showing Him that He alone was worthy to be preeminent over all other human relationships and obligations. Mary knew that Christ's time on earth was limited. She chose the "good part," that of spending time with Him personally. By doing so she heard wonderful words of commendation from His blessed lips. Those words assured her that this part would never be taken away from her.

We need to follow Mary's example. As women, it's much easier for most of us to talk to Him, giving Him all of our complaints, than it is to listen to what He has to say to us. He would help us with our struggles of being overworked, not appreciated, or any other serious complaint we may have. In fellowship at His feet, we would find our best answers of balance as we arrange our time and priorities in worship, service, and fellowship. I need have no worry that devotion and worship to Jesus Christ will hinder my service for Him in any way. In fact, the more I know Him the easier it is to serve Him as my love for Him will deepen.

50
WHAT'S IN A NAME?

How would you like to have been given the name "Little Devil"? It's hard to imagine any mother giving her innocent baby a name like that, but soon after our arrival in China we met a ten-year old boy with this name. Frankly, I was shocked. When I asked him if his mother had a special reason for choosing that name, he said, "Yes," and explained that all Oriental names had meaning. His mother, who loved him, had wanted to protect him from evil spirits so she had chosen that name in the hopes that the evil spirits would not think of her little boy as being a special treasure to her and spirit him away. (This common practice in those days gave us insight into the Chinese culture and how much superstition governed their private lives.)

We liked him and hired him to be our goat boy. As parents of a two-year-old who were expecting a second baby in a land of few dairy products, we had no choice but to raise our own goats. Raising goats, in turn, necessitated hiring a boy to take them up into the mountains every day to scrounge for food. To give us a better feeling, we decided to call our youngster, "Small Sunshine," which sounded similar to "Little Devil" in Chinese. We thought the name suited him because he was happy and outgoing.

Less than a year after hiring our goat boy, we were walking past a pawn shop in town when a camera in the shop window caught our eye. We recognized the camera as exactly the same as ours and were surprised to see a price tag on it. We stopped to question the owner of the shop about it. Once inside, we found several other items belonging to us. Our inquiry revealed that a young boy had brought in all of those items. Although we had been missing various objects at an alarming rate, we never once suspected our innocent-looking, likable ray of sunshine as being a thief.

Although he had not been too young to steal, our goat boy had been too young to think things through and cover up his theft. He had registered all our items in his own name, so he was easily proven guilty. We didn't press charges, however, because we hoped to help him. Gifford tried to get him to understand that stealing was wrong, but to no avail. Finally we had to release him from his duties because more and more items were disappearing. When even our linens and curtains began disappearing, we realized "Little Sunshine" was not working alone. We could not prove that he was the culprit and had stolen all of the missing things, but there was little doubt as to who was responsible. We began to wonder if he had not been rightly named after all.

When thinking of names, Revelation 2:17 came to mind. John mentioned that when Christ returns, He will give a white stone to each person who believes in Him. In the stone a new name will be written. When babies are named, parents look ahead into the future. However, at Christ's return, our names will summarize our past lives on earth. Our new names will express what He thinks of our lives.

I wonder how He will sum up my life with one word. What name will He pick to express my character or actions on earth? There are several words from which I sincerely hope He will choose; patience, hope, faith, or consolation. I can think of no greater reward than seeing pleasure in His eyes and a warm smile on His face as He hands me my new name. It will be like receiving an award or diploma at the end of good service. I hope with all my heart that He will be well-pleased and that I will receive an honorable name when He evaluates my life.

51
WHAT SHALL WE DO?

The story written for us in Judges 13:2-14 gives us insight into the heart of Samson's parents as they waited for a child. Just how long they waited we don't know, but it was long enough to cause them real concern. In addition to their personal desire, Samson's mother suffered reproach from her neighbors and friends because she was barren. Knowing the culture of those days and the necessity of keeping the ancestral line intact, we can sympathize with her. There is nothing like thinking you can't give birth to a baby to make a woman want to become a mother all the more. The desire to hold her own offspring in her arms easily becomes an obsession. I know because I waited more than three years for my first little girl.

The reaction of Samson's parents to the angel's wonderful announcement promising the birth of their son reveals their character. Their first reaction was not one of selfish love or personal gratification, but rather an honest desire to learn how to rear the child in a way that would please God and assure a mature, godly adult. They first asked the angel, in effect, "What shall we do? What shall we teach him?" These questions revealed their strong feelings of responsibility toward God for rearing the new life that would be entrusted to their care.

The angel's answer was perhaps surprising. His instructions were extremely simple. He offered no long discourse on child training, nor gave them any special "how-to" books to read. He merely gave Samson's mother what to us would seem to be unrelated and rather strange commands. He reminded her to keep Samson from drinking alcoholic drinks and to not cut the child's hair. He was to eat nothing unclean according to Jewish law. He was to be brought up from birth as a Nazarite and his mother was to begin from his conception practicing the same restrictions on food and drink. They seem to me to be too strict for a small child, yet the boy was to practice total abstinence. All of this would require strong discipline and careful supervision on the part of his parents.

In this story, we find a few basic principles for rearing children that we would do well to follow today. These instructions apply to anyone who is entrusted with the training of children in general such as Sunday school teachers, nursery-care providers, and school teachers. The circle widens to include single people who are aunts, friends, and neighbors. This is especially true of grandparents. Each one has a strong influence on the young lives that surround them.

I am eternally grateful to one such woman who influenced my life during a crucial time of decision. During my sophomore year of high school, my mother became very sick and required surgery, so I offered to manage the home and care for my baby brother who was fifteen years my junior. I did this for two years, during which time I began dating a worldly-wise man seven years my senior. When he spoke of marriage, my heart heartily agreed and I was severely tempted to forget my high school education to begin a home of my own. But just at that time, I became friendly with a widow in our neighborhood. She would invite me to sit on her porch and, holding cups of tea, we would talk. She recognized the turn my life was taking, so she strongly encouraged me to finish my schooling rather than enter into a premature marriage. Naturally, my parents advised the same thing, but it didn't have the same effect as the persuasion of this loving, understanding woman. I shudder now when I think how different my life would be today had I not followed her wise advice.

When God entrusts us with a little person, who has a personality and character that needs training, we need to think about how we can best accomplish that training. Feeling our responsibility to teach our children separation from the world, we need to strongly emphasize self-control and obedience. The earlier we start to train our children's appetites to refrain from many things commonly consumed by the world but harmful to our spiritual life, the better. I'm sure Samson heard many times, from early childhood on, that he was to be separated for God to use and that he was to demonstrate his self-discipline by keeping himself from the ways of the Gentiles around him.

In child training, Proverbs 24:30-34 also comes to mind. The physical and material teaching is obvious in these verses, but we know that the principle is the same in the spiritual realm. We need to put as much emphasis on spiritual development as we do on physical development. *"I went by the field of the slothful,"* Solomon writes, *"and lo, it was all grown over with thorns...and the stone wall thereof was broken down."* This describes all the fruit of the curse. If we do not teach our children to keep the weeds of sin pulled and the stone walls of protection repaired, wild beasts will enter freely and consume what little fruit there is. Our children can learn early that growing a beautiful garden in their lives can only be done through hard work.

Let me add a few words of comfort to those parents who, to the best of their ability, have done all the right things in teaching their children self-control and obedience and yet their children have chosen a different path. In spite of the fact that Samson's parents adhered strictly to God's instructions, Samson was far from a model young person when he reached adulthood. Samson chose his own lifestyle. I'm sure his parents shed many tears while watching him learn to follow God the hard way. In Hebrews 11:32, I have been encouraged to see Samson's name listed with three men of faith. His faith helped him through the final tragic moments of his life when he called on the Lord. I am comforted to know that in the end of his life Samson turned to God. When he prayed in faith for God's strength, he accomplished more through his death than he did through his lifetime (Jud. 16: 28-30).

52
WOMEN PRIESTS

For the last few days I have been preparing a lesson on the tabernacle, and my mind has been occupied with the activities of the Old Testament priests. I've been captivated by the beauty of their clothes, especially the ephod and the breastplate. All the colorful gems and golden threads must have been absolutely gorgeous. One thing I have noticed is that God instructed that each garment be tied at the shoulders, making a one-size-fits-all garment that could be passed down from one generation to the next. The same garment would fit a large person as well as a slightly built person.

Correlating the duties of those priests to our duties as priests of God today, I have learned much about my obligations as a woman priest. Both 1 Peter 2:5 and Revelation 1:5-6 remind me of my spiritual privileges and support the truth that we Christian women are priests. *"Ye also, as living stones,"* Peter writes, *"are built up a spiritual house, an holy priesthood, to offer up spiritual sacrifices, acceptable to God by Jesus Christ."* John writes, *"Jesus Christ...hath made us kings and priests unto God and His Father; to Him be glory and dominion for ever and ever. Amen."*

The priests of the Old Testament had great responsibilities, but if we think honestly, don't we have equally important and exacting duties? Just as the priest's first and foremost occupation was to worship God by offering sacrifices to Him, John 4:23 tells us that God still desires our worship. Psalm 69:30-31 gives us a hint of how we can do this. *"I will praise the name of God with a song, and will magnify Him with thanks-*

giving. This also shall please the Lord better than an ox or bullock." We offer worship, praise, and thanksgiving to God for His Son, the Lord Jesus Christ. When Joseph sent his brothers back to Canaan to tell his father that he was still alive, he reminded them to tell Jacob all about his present glory as a ruler in Egypt. God also revels in hearing about His Son.

The Old Testament offerings were pretty costly, and sometimes the offerings God requires of us are equally expensive. Giving thanks when we aren't happy about our circumstances and offering the daily sacrifice of living a righteous life in the midst of a polluted world often exact a high price. Also, a life of prayer on behalf of the people of God is time-consuming labor that easily becomes a real battle. Special incense, made to order, lifted the priest's prayers heavenward. Today, instead of incense, the precious name of God's beloved Son bears our adoration and petitions heavenward. His name is always a sweet fragrance to His Father.

As mother priests, we must intercede for our children regardless of their ages. We must never underestimate the influence of a godly mother's intercessory prayers for a son or daughter, nor should we ever become so discouraged that we give up praying for them.

In the same way, single-sister priests have an obligation to intercede in a special way for other single people who struggle with problems that are best known by another single. This involves praying for them and showing as much interest in them as if they were family members. We may also intercede for the host of friends and family members who have not yet received Christ as Lord. Who can evaluate the importance of any of these functions?

Another office of an Old Testament priest involved encouragement:

> *"And it shall be, when ye are come nigh unto the battle, that the priest shall approach and speak unto the people, and*

shall say,…let not your hearts faint, fear not, and do not tremble, neither be ye terrified because of them; for the Lord your God is He that goeth with you, to fight for you against your enemies, to save you" (Deut. 20:2-4).

Many a heart becomes discouraged, disappointed and fearful. It is our responsibility to go before the Lord and receive the right word of encouragement to pass on to those who are bogged down in spiritual warfare. By keeping our spiritual morale high, we can make sure that we do not spread infectious, negative attitudes that will discourage others rather than build them up.

Last, but certainly not least, we have the privilege of standing as priests between a righteous God and His sinful people. Not only do we intercede on their behalf, but we also represent God to the sinful people who surround us daily, carefully giving them a balanced view of God's holiness and great love and mercy. Surely the whole function of evangelization by His priests lies heavily on the heart of God, who is not willing that any should perish but that all should come to repentance.

Envisioning myself in the beautiful high-priestly robes with all the gems and gold, and feeling the importance of the office of a priest, gives me a new appreciation of my high and holy calling. They make me feel very special before God. Knowing that I am clothed with the gorgeous robes of Christ's righteousness keeps me from being prideful because my beauty in Christ is no more to my credit than the beauty of Old Testament priests' garments was to theirs.

53
WOMEN'S INFLUENCE ON CHILDREN

When the princess of Egypt found Miriam's baby brother, Moses, in the river where his mother had hidden him, Miriam suggested that she find a nursemaid for him. According to the plan of God, the princess agreed to the idea and Miriam soon brought her mother, Jochebed, to be interviewed for the position. The princess hired her, and Jochebed received wages for nursing her own child. Can you imagine how happy she was? I'm sure she would gladly have paid for such a privilege. She had the joy of watching her baby grow. By the time he became an adult, she had been able to instill in him the ability to choose by faith to leave the palace and all of its prestige and comfort. She saw the results of her home training when, as a young man, he actually preferred to *"suffer affliction with the people of God, than to enjoy the pleasures of sin for a season"* (Heb. 11:25).

Jochebed saw the reward of the time and effort she put into Moses' life. So will we, if we are faithful to our children (or anyone else's children, for that matter). Children around us are subject to many voices that clamor for their ears—such as T.V., movies, ungodly school teachers, and their peers.

Seldom, sad to say, are those good influences. Knowing this, God commands us to *"gather...children...that they may hear, and that they may learn, and fear the Lord your God, and observe to do all the words of this law"* (Deut. 31:12). In obedience to His command, I'm sure that if we were more aware of our opportunities, we'd find many ways to gather children to nurse for the Lord. All the while praying for God's guidance, we need to instill in children a desire for God and a love for His Word. Such a desire is far more important than a desire to live only for their own gratification. I recall at least three women of God who gathered me to themselves at some point in my life and did this for me.

My mother was the one whom God used most often to influence me. Mother gathered us at night for bedtime stories, which were a time of constant learning. Her firm faith and quiet peace under various circumstances calmed many a fear and continue to this day to positively challenge me. I can only remember a few stormy days during the early teens when I felt negative feelings toward her.

I well remember a time when I was eight years old. She was tucking me in for the night, and when she bent down to kiss me, I asked her in all seriousness, "Mother, who will I marry? You married Daddy, but how will I find a man to marry?" I still have a clear memory of her response. She told me that only God had the answer to that question, then suggested that we begin praying every night that when "Mr. Right" came along I would recognize him and that I would not marry "Mr. Wrong" before "Mr. Right" came. From that night on, we prayed this request together and rarely forgot it. God certainly answered our prayer.

A dear Sunday school teacher gathered children together not only on Sunday mornings but at other times as well. She thought of many excuses for activities, all with the purpose of teaching us to fear the Lord. One Saturday afternoon, at a party in her home, she asked me outright if I was saved. At the time, I answered in the affirmative, but I knew well in my heart that I was not. Her question started my thinking about the condition of my spiritual life, which later led to my conversion. In spite of my seeming disinterest at the time, I was drawn by her love for the Lord and for me. She always stressed the importance of being ready for the imminent return of the Lord.

196

Then in high school, I had a history teacher who I knew was a Christian. Although she was austere and in a measure she intimidated me, I still would visit her before or after school. I'm sure this was because she always offered a listening ear, making me feel welcome. I often shared doubts and fears with her that I was embarrassed to mention to my parents. Although I didn't always appreciate her answers and the abundant advice she offered, I knew she loved me and I was drawn to her.

Time spent with children and young people is never wasted if there is good input of Christian values and morals. The kind touch of his aunt's loving hand on my husband's shoulder at Bible camp planted the seed of missionary service in his heart. Years later, in deep gratitude, he often referred to this gentle coaxing. He often attributed the complete change in the direction of his life during his late teens to his dear missionary aunt.

We must be consistent in teaching our youth to discern the voice of God from the voices of the world by teaching them to fear God. They need to learn how, by reading God's Word, to tell the difference between the truth of the Living God and the teachings of the many strange gods of this world.

Certainly women who hold the truth of God firmly are most influential in the lives of our youth. We can encourage ourselves by thinking of Jochebed. Her wages for her services were threefold. At the time she raised Moses, she received monetary reward. Later on, she had the joy of watching him mature spiritually. Finally, she has yet to receive her best reward when God will pay her His wages for childcare. Believe me, He will not pay minimum wage, either, for He gives in abundant measure, *"pressed down, and shaken together, and running over"* (Luke 6:38).